CHIN MUSIC

A Collection of Columns, and Other Musings

By Bill Bielecky

Neil,
A toast to the
Woodpecker — Chins
up!
Bill B

The columns in this book are based on true events. Or actual dreams. No names have been changed to protect the innocent. Nobody is really innocent anyway. The emails are figments of the imagination, please bring your own. The poems are plausibly deniable. Read on at your own risk.

For Cindy Vance Bielecky, my most subtle editor.

In memory of Mom, Patricia Bielecky,
always my biggest fan.

The following people I thank profusely:

James Abraham, one of my favorite editors, I often
cringed in horror as he scalpelled my stuff, only to
find later how much better it was.

Hillary Ring, my funniest editor, who proofed
many of the columns and was instrumental
in helping me publish this collection.

"This is why people OD on pills,
and jump from the Golden Gate Bridge.
Anything to feel weightless again."

Table of Contents

Table of Contents

Table of Contents

THE WOODPECKER FAN CLUB

INTRO

When I was a kid, I hated Don Drysdale. I watched a lot of sports with my Dad, and at that age I usually adopted his views on team loyalties and individual player preferences, like any eight-year old boy. One afternoon while we were watching a Dodgers game my old man said, "Drysdale is a head-hunter." That was it. I never liked Don Drysdale the rest of his career.

Funny thing though, I loved Juan Marichal. And Bob Gibson. Nolan Ryan, Roger Clemens – no problem. Those guys just threw a little chin music now and then to remind hitters not to dig in. Drysdale hunted heads. Which of course he didn't. I don't think.

***

Most of the columns in this collection were published by either the Tallahassee Democrat, or the Gadsden County Times. True behemoths of the opinion column industry. Following each column I have included the date it was written or published, and I have identified the publications of columns I can verify, but for many of them

I don't have anything to remember me by, other than the words on the page. My first column for the Gadsden County Times was published October 2, 1997, my last was July 7, 1998. All columns between those dates were likely published in the GCT, unless otherwise noted.

I was never paid by the Tallahassee Democrat. You'd think I was a Republican or something. The Gadsden County Times rewarded me with a $15.00 paycheck for (almost) every column I submitted. The column titled "Songs From the Bad Chair" was also published in Big Apple Parent (May 1999), which paid me $20, if memory serves. I gave my Mom, who was my agent at the time, no commission whatsoever. She remained my agent anyway.

My first published column occurred shortly after I graduated law school in December, 1996. At the time, the only thing I was sure of was that I did not want to be a lawyer (I'm still sure). A few months later Tiger Woods won the Masters with an iconic, historic performance. And Fuzzy Zoeller said to cameras pointing right at him that Tiger should not order fried chicken for the Masters' dinner the following year. "Or, collard greens or whatever the hell they eat." I wrote "Whistling Dixie?" a few days later, and with absolutely no invitation or encouragement, I sent my freshly inked piece to an editor of the Tallahassee Democrat, James Abraham. I expected nothing, unless it was a cookie-cutter rejection saying thanks but no thanks. I had submitted stuff to publishers before.

Within an hour I got a call from James Abraham inviting me to come to the Democrat and discuss my column. James was enthusiastic and welcoming. He published my column in the Friday paper that week. So, I abandoned the idea of the law profession, which was not exactly recruiting me, and started writing opinion columns. Thank you, James.

Now, about the Chin Music thing. In the fall of 1997, James suggested I talk to the Gadsden County Times about doing a weekly column. The editors of the GC Times asked me to come up with a byline for the column. Something catchy, clever, or insightful to my style. I settled on Chin Music. I'm no Don Drysdale. I tried not to throw at anyone's head intentionally, although maybe a column or two just got away from me. (Sorry, Fuzzy.) But hopefully some of my columns backed a few people off the plate a bit.

* * *

I have included a section titled "Woodpecker Fan Club." The WFC was a series of emails I wrote to fellow teachers and administrators when I was teaching at John I. Leonard High School in Lake Worth, Florida. A brief explanation of how the WFC came about prefaces the emails.

* * *

I have included a section for my poems also. I'm sorry. But the main reason I'm putting my musings into this publication is so my kids have an idea of who their father was, or at least, how he thought when he took the time to think, back before they knew me. So, while my poems may seem both sophomoric at times and esoteric beyond comprehension at others, please be assured that I know exactly what I was saying almost fifty percent of the time. The rest is just elementary poetry, make of it what you will. Sometimes I just like the ways certain words sound.

* * *

Since the majority of these columns (and other musings) are over twenty years old, you might notice how things have changed in the world since I wrote them. On the other hand, an awful lot of the topics I ruminated on seem to insist that things have changed very little. Race relations? Status quo with 1997, I'd say. The pestilence meter I wrote about in "The Good News About Bad News?" Well, let's just say, thou shalt not Covid thy neighbor right about now. Or his wife. And hurricane season is nigh upon us, if the wildfires and locusts don't get us first. And Tiger just won another Masters! But without any Fuzzy comments to make us slap our knees this time. Oh, well. I bet Fuzz was whistling somewhere. But not anywhere near Dixie. Or a camera.

Ok then. Pull your helmet on nice and tight, and waggle your bat. But don't dig your cleats in too deep. Chins up, let the music play.

THE COLUMNS

"There's too much chin music an' too little fightin' in this war, anyhow"

- Stephen Crane, *Red Badge of Courage*

Whistling Dixie?

I am not Tiger Woods. Really, I'm not. Sometimes, just before I hit a shot, when I am seeing only good things happening to the ball, I cry out inside, "I am Tiger Woods!" But the ball gives me away. It does not go that far or that straight. And my skin gives me away too. It's not that dark. I am not black, which is a genetic insignificance when claiming to be Tiger if you believe one large sponsor's ads. But, no. I am really not Tiger Woods.

But, if I was Tiger Woods. Oh, baby, if I was Tiger Woods. Here's what I would do. I would not accept Fuzzy Zoeller's apology. No way. I would tell the old jokester to take a long walk on a short island green. I would tell him to open wide and see how many Big Bertha drivers would fit into the yap of the PGA's funnyman. I would hire Mojo Nixon to write a song called "Fuzzy Zoeller Must Die." I would have Mojo reserve a verse or two for Fred Couples, and Tom Lehman, and any other professional golfer who attempts to play down the Fuzzster's comments.

Ah, the Fuzzster. What a fun guy. He whistles when he plays golf tournaments that are worth hundreds of thousands of dollars. I can't find musical notes on my keyboard, but if I could I would insert them here. Whistle whistle whistle. What is that tune he whistles, anyway?

Fuzzy jokes with the spectators at golf tournaments. Fuzzy's name is Fuzzy. He must be a likable guy. He must be a funny guy. Funny Fuzzy. Sounds like a very marketable children's toy. But Fuzzy has recently volunteered his life's accomplishments – and a life-size photo of his own mouth with seventy-two golf balls in it – to the Wall of Shame.

Here is what Fuzzy did. He looked into a network's lens (the camera never blinks, remember, Fuzzy?) at this year's Masters and spoke the most incredible words. On the eve of golf's most historical win of all time, at the most prestigious of all golf tournaments – deep in the heart of Dixie – in a region where very likely more black men have hung from trees than have played rounds at this hallowed course, Fuzzy called Tiger Woods "that little boy," and mentioned fried chicken and collard greens in the same breath. How did he forget watermelons?

Quicker than a downhill putt at Augusta, this well-loved, respected golf professional wriggled his Fuzzy legacy between the likes of Al Campanis and Jimmy "the Greek" Snyder. Fuzzy played the race card. Vincent Bugliosi must be upset. But, he should not be, because Fuzzy apologized. Fuzzy said he did not mean for the comments to be taken in a racial context. Really? Then I bet Fuzzy said the same things about Greg Norman last year after three rounds at the Masters. Norman was so confused by the remarks that he hit seven balls in the water and barely broke a hundred in the final round.

Fuzzy not only apologized for his recent quips, he also made it clear that he has been on the tour for twenty-three years and has always been known as a jokester. He forgot to mention that some of his best friends were jokes. But some of his PGA buddies did remember. Tom Lehman, the recently anointed number one golfer in the world – and therefore worthy of extracting a quick quote from on controversial issues – said that it was obvious that Fuzzy was trying to be funny. Maybe Lehman thinks this video should end up on golf bloopers. Because he did say the comments were unfortunate coming in the midst of a landmark event in golf history.

Hey, Tom. When would the remarks not be unfortunate? At a celebrity roast of Ted Danson, maybe?

But Lehman also said that Fuzzy probably would have said the same thing to Tiger's face, and the two would have "yukked" it up. Hello. Would somebody please slap this man? Is Lehman suggesting that this is what professional golfers do on the tee boxes while waiting for the group in front to clear? Tell off-color ethnic jokes?

"Hey, Tiger, you know why blacks don't drive convertibles?"

"I heard that one, Fuzzy." Yuk, yuk.

"Well, then, you know how many Chinamen it takes to – oh, she's Thai? Yuk, yuk."

All this time I thought they were discussing yardages, pin placements, and wind variables. Professional golf is more fun than I thought.

But wait. There's more. Fred Couples also weighed in a few clubs short of the green. Couples stressed that Tiger is treated the same as any other golfer on the tour. Mighty white of the guys, eh? Couples added that off-the-wall comments were made all the time, and that there was nothing racist about these particular comments. He SAID "We don't have any problems like that out here." We're going to have to bring in canned yuks here; I just can't make myself do it.

I have only one question for Fred. Out where? Does he mean out there on the lily-white PGA tour? No, I don't guess there were any problems when all the white guys used to get together every weekend and chase rich purses and richer sponsorships. For years Fuzzy has been standing just off the green while someone like Davis Love III putted for the lead. Fuzzy would whisper to the cameras, "If he makes it, tell him we don't want no fried chicken – or whatever the hell it is his people serve." And the spectators would go, "Yuk, yuk, yuk." And none of the white guys on tour would be bothered at all. Davis Love I and II might not yuk, but no one else cared.

Fuzzy Zoeller might as well have looked into the camera that day at the Masters and said, "Dammit, this here's Augusta, and there's a nigger in the woodpile!" It would have been no more or less racist than what he did say. If you are going to smack the world in the face with your ignorance, you should do it in style. You should not leave yourself a clever escape route such as the "misconstrued" and "merely joking" routines. You should be able to look at yourself in the mirror in the morning and know exactly what kind of person you are. Anybody who saw the video knows.

Fred Couples says he does not think it's a big deal, and he does not think Tiger will either. But I think it is a big deal. And I hope Tiger does too. I hope he does not let the cleated feet slide easily out of Zoeller's mouth and let this go away real fast. Somebody out there needs to stand up and say what this really is. Zoeller would be a nice start.

Several weeks ago Fuzzy's good friend, John Daly, checked into an alcohol abuse rehabilitation facility. The cameras also caught up with Fuzzy the day after Daly's last publicized binge. As I recall his words, Zoeller stated that late the night before he had seen Daly in his inebriated condition, and suggested that he had seen a man (Daly) at his lowest possible point. When Fuzzy sees the video of his Master's comments; when he looks in the mirror; I wonder what he sees.

They are going to try to teach John Daly how to admit to and cope with his problem, with his sickness. If there is a clinic for racism out there it's time for Fuzzy to go tell it on his own mountain. It's time for the game of golf to check itself in.

Tallahassee Democrat - April 25, 1997

Crying Wolfe

You need a good reason to live in north Florida? Go visit south Florida. You think the panhandle has the warm climate you would like to live in, but is a cultural Kalahari? Are you afraid that Tallahassee traffic is just one more vehicle from permanent lockjaw? Tired of all the environmentalists crying about trees and lakes and birds? You want to be able to hit the open highway and put the speedometer needle over the top occasionally? You should move to south Florida. Everyone else has.

I went home again last week for a visit. I elbowed my way back into the city where I lived for thirty-three of my thirty-eight years. Twice I have moved from the West Palm Beach area to Tallahassee to seek higher education and to see the azaleas bloom. So far, I have only moved back once. Thomas Wolfe whispered to me then. He is shouting at me now.

The ugliness of south Florida emerges slowly as you travel the turnpike, like a junkyard in the morning fog.

Somewhere below Orlando you begin to notice that the grass does not grow as nicely on the sides of the road. The wildflowers quietly disappear. Closer to West Palm Beach you will notice that native trees like slash pines, oaks, and cypress have been replaced by homely invasions of Brazilian pepper, Australian pines, and melaleuca. Grass has turned to weeds. Welcome home.

There is no mistaking the lack of aesthetic appeal of the landscape that is peculiar to this part of Florida. Compared to Tallahassee, West Palm and the surrounding cities are like a giant footprint in the flower garden. Tallahassee faces occasional traffic gridlock partly because the massive oaks that canvas some streets are protected, thereby preventing road widening. There are no canopied roads in south Florida. The only deterrent there to the ever-widening of roads is other roads that they might encroach upon. Some roads are so wide the crosswalks need names.

I-95 in south Florida is double-ugly. The roadside is xeriscaped nicely with sand, weeds, and chunks of rubber tires. It is the Dodge City of highways; a crazed renegade sector of interstate. Reckless driving is not a violation there – it's a requirement. I hesitate in fear when I enter the on-ramp, the way I do before getting on a steeply declining escalator with my arms full of packages.

There are no real trees left down south. Palm trees are mascots, not arbor. Shade is provided only by the tall buildings that have been built along every inch of the beachfronts that have attracted so many people. In order to see the beachfronts you have to be in the tall buildings.

Southeast Florida is a flat and barren terrain. Hills are extinct. I grew up about two blocks from a slight land elevation that we affectionately referred to as a hill. It was the only one around. When the I-95 extension came through, construction workers barricaded the elevation with large trucks and jackhammered for weeks and weeks. When they moved the trucks the land was flat. They pancaked our hill.

The only reminders of what south Florida once was are the names of the developments that erased it all. Quail Ridge. Fox Run. Bear Lakes. This is whimsical waxing, because the names lie. There may be a lake or two, but you're pushing it if you are looking for a ridge. The quail are on someone's plate. "Fox Run!" is something the developers yelled just before they broke ground. Jack Nicklaus will have to do if you want to see a bear.

The developments have nice houses, though. So nice that they make them all look the same. Then they smash them real close together and paint them the same color. Take a number. And don't forget it, because it's the only way to find your own house.

Culturally, south Florida is well endowed. Cultural events in Tallahassee include bird watching, butterfly gardening, and mulching the azalea hedge. South Florida does not have the time nor the ingredients for these activities. There are operas, concerts, art festivals, plays, and black-tie cocktail parties to attend. If you want to see a bird you can drive to a K-mart parking lot before they open in the morning and feed the flocks of seagulls who have long ago given up on the ocean as a source for food.

There are not many butterflies in south Florida either. Occasionally you get lucky and squash a stray with your windshield. There are no plant-a-tree days like Tallahassee has. They do not necessarily have enough water to sustain the burgeoning population of humans. South Floridians know that trees drink the water that could be used for a magnificent fountain that will make some tall new building that is blocking the ocean look good.

In Tallahassee there is often litigation and protests accompanying new developments or wider roads. Some people want to save the trees and the lakes. Others want to prevent more traffic in their neighborhood. There do not appear to be any more trees or lakes to fight over in West Palm Beach. When more cars come, they will add a lane or two to the roads. If Thomas Wolfe was right – if you can't go home again – then south Florida is a good place to be from.

Tallahassee Democrat - May 18, 1997

Joe Camel's Kids

Looks like they're going to arrest Joe Camel. Put 'em up, humpback. And take off those child-seducing shades before we slap them off you. Joe is just too cool. His existence is clearly a violation of moral turpitude worthy of inducing public outrage and scorn. And a bunch of lawsuits. We're gonna get you, sucker.

R.J. Reynolds Tobacco Co. – the parental unit of Joe Camel – is being charged with illegally inducing children to smoke. Proof of this crime is: a) kids smoke; and b) there are Joe Camel cartoon ads that run on billboards and in magazines. The ads don't mention kids, or depict children smoking. But, if a kid looked where a Joe Camel ad was placed, the kid might be illegally induced to smoke a cigarette because the cartoon character is sooooo cool.

The Federal Trade Commission is all over these slicksters at RJR. The FTC's director of the Bureau of Consumer Protection exposed the fiendish plot of the tobacco mongrels. She explained that cartoons have a particular appeal to children. So do bugs, mud, and bellybuttons, but apparently none of these are inducing kids to smoke. No, it's cartoon characters like Joe Camel who are persuading the kids. But if a bug – say, a cricket – were to be the mascot for something like cigarette lighters, then the badges would have to flash again, wouldn't they?

Sorry about that, Cricket. But they were going to be on to you soon anyway. In Cricket's defense, it should be noted that some kids don't use lighters to light cigarettes. Sometimes they use them to start small fires that end up burning down apartment complexes. Stick 'em up Jiminy.

Maybe the best way to test the FTC's logic is to apply the "cool cartoon character" theory to other products. If their hypothesis holds up then lots of youngsters must be buying life insurance policies. Who is cooler than Snoopy, the Metropolitan Life representative? And Dow-Corning must have been handing out rolls of fiberglass insulation like lollipops at the bank drive-through when the Pink Panther was pitching the itchy stuff.

I think Joe is getting a bum rap here. I think kids were smoking cigs way before a cartoon camel put sunglasses on. Lots of kids have puffed coffin nails and then become adults and tried to stop the next generation of kids from puffing. The whole silly cycle would be pretty boring if we didn't invent a new whipping boy every so often. So Joe Camel has to take the fall.

But if we are going to start using this "illegally

inducing" theory, why don't we go after the real bad guys.

I mean, Nicole Brown Simpson and Ron Goldman had their throats sliced. Why are there no charges against the knifemaker for illegally inducing a well-known celebrity into carving up two people minding their own business? I think knives have a particular appeal to big guys who want to kill people quietly.

Some toddlers are using their parents for target practice. And I keep reading about shoot-outs in schoolyards. Can't the gun manufacturers be booked for inducing kids to cap their moms, dads, and each other for lunch money?

No, I don't suppose the FTC can get the firearm folks, because they don't advertise with a cartoon character carrying a pistol on his hip. But if the FTC ever finds the person who drew up Elmer Fudd, or Yosemite Sam, or Johnny Quest....

Tallahassee Democrat - June 8, 1997

What Came First, Ethics Or the Dilemma?

I'm having an ethical dilemma. Morals, ethics, and values are very confusing for me. The problem is that I don't know what ethics are. They are not tangible things. I looked up the word in the dictionary and I still don't know what they are. The dictionary says something about a system of moral principles and a philosophy of right and wrong. So, I had to look up morals, too. Conforming to the principles of right conduct. Ooohh, doesn't sound much like me. No wonder I get in so much trouble.

It appears to me that ethics are just a bunch of rules made up by somebody who didn't like anyone but himself. For some reason we try really hard to follow these rules. That's why America is so full of people who don't like anyone but themselves.

How did we get this way? It seems that an awful lot of the moral fiber we are supposed to swallow comes from religious sources. Thou shalt NOT! There are many people in this country who believe in the Thou Shalt Nots.

And if thou shalt, it can often lead to thou's arrest. So this is the ethical dilemma the country faces. Because we shalt a lot more than we should.

People who violate our society's ethical code can be prosecuted, court martialed, or shunned. Clearly, if you kill someone, you will be prosecuted. Unless you had a good reason for killing someone. Like someone tried to kill you first, or someone beat you senseless for many years until you couldn't take it anymore. If you have a self-defense or battered-syndrome theory working for you our society might just forget that Thou Shalt Not Kill. But if you premeditated the killing and have no extenuating circumstance theory to ply, then our society will probably kill you. Very confusing.

Thou should also not commit adultery. But if you can't help yourself and you get caught, society will cluck its tongue and shake its head at you. Unless you are in the military, because then you can get court-martialed. In the military they train you how to kill people that you never met. In case we go to war. If we do go to war and you kill a lot of people you don't know, society may call you a hero. But if the Navy catches you cheating on your wife you can go to jail.

Apparently, thou shalt not be a homosexual either. I don't remember this on the original list of Thou Shalt Nots, but it seems to rank in the top ten these days. If you are a homosexual our society can turn its back on you and pretend you don't exist. Legally. Like if you apply for a job and say, yes, I am gay. Or if you want to marry someone you love, honor, and cherish. Our society probably believes that thou shalt not kill homosexuals, but it's unclear where we stand on beating a few up on a fun Saturday night.

The military decided to no longer shun homosexuals by adopting a "don't ask, don't tell" policy. However, if you tell you can still be tossed out. There doesn't seem to be any penalty for asking. And I don't really know what happens if we go to war and a homosexual kills a lot of people he doesn't know and then "tells" at his ticker tape parade.

Southern Baptists know what to do about homosexuals. Boycott Disney! Disney must go to family values purgatory because they extended company benefits to partners of homosexual employees, and because they produce "Ellen." If enough Southern Baptists don't spend any Disney-dollars the company might feel financially burdened and get back in line with society by denying the benefits and canceling "Ellen." Lots of people might be hurt by this coercive tactic, but that appears a small price to pay for restoring morality to our great land.

Mike Bowers' interpretation of morals and ethics is even more confusing. Bowers also knew what to do with homosexuals. Prosecute them for sodomy and deny them jobs in his office. That is what Bowers did during his tenure as Georgia's Attorney General. But Bowers didn't know what to do about adulterers. He recently admitted that he was an adulterer for ten years while he was in office. He admitted it because lots of people already knew about it.

No charges were ever filed against Attorney General Bowers, although adultery is against the law in Georgia. And Bowers did not lose his job because of his affair. He did resign from the Air National Guard because of it, though. The potential for a court-martial was probably a bit unsettling. Especially since it could interfere with Bowers' candidacy for governor. If only he had killed a bunch of people he didn't know while he was in the military. Then he could fall back on that.

Tallahassee Democrat - July 6, 1997

The Duke of Secrecy

It must be a promoter's nightmare. David Duke is coming to Tallahassee, but he can't say where he will speak. Tickets are ten bucks, and the discussion topics are affirmative action and illegal immigration. But just where the ex-big cheese of the KKK will expound on these issues is a mystery, and it will stay that way until noon on Saturday.

Saturday at noon is when you can start calling any one of three hotline numbers to find out where the old wizard will appear. Quite suspenseful, isn't it? Kind of adds a little touch of danger and intrigue to the otherwise uneventful event. After all, how exciting could a David Duke discussion of affirmative action and illegal immigration be? His stance on these topics will not be nearly as surprising as the location of the delivery will be.

But, in spite of the special atmosphere created by the cloak of secrecy, I still don't know if I want to shell out the money before I know where the dragonmeister is going to be. What if I ante up early and then find the hotlines all jammed up with eager Dukies all day? Or, what if it turns out the speech will take place in a cornfield thirty miles outside of town?

Even if I did know the location beforehand, I'm not sure I would want to attend. They might have a Left-Wing-Troublemaker scanning device at the door. They would probably nab me even without the advanced technology. They'd spot me because I don't have a swastika tattoo or a shaved head. No iron cross earrings. They would stomp me like a ripe grape when I didn't laugh loudly enough at a "Mallard Filmore" cartoon they make everyone read.

No, I'm not going. Just talked myself right out of it. David Duke is just too dangerous. He's probably going to undo in one night all the good things the mayor of Tallahassee and the President of the United States have done for race relations recently. He's probably going to whip an overflowing crowd into a Confederate-flag-waving, cross-burning, heil-Hitlering frenzy. Old hatreds will flare, new battle lines will be drawn, the streets will run red with the blood of....

Whoa! Sorry, got stuck in a John Grisham novel for a second. But you can see what kind of emotional tantrums Duke can inspire just by being here and not telling us where he will be. Maybe his promoter is much smarter than I thought. And maybe they should take the secrecy thing one step further next time. Because you can only wonder what kind of madness would reign if he didn't tell us where he would be, or what he would speak about. Or if he never told us he was coming at all.

Tallahassee Democrat – July 18, 1997

Oz And Them

Most movies go well with a large bucket of popcorn and a soda you can barely get your hand around. This simply won't do for a screening of "The Wizard of Oz" with Pink Floyd's "Dark Side of the Moon" overlaid as a soundtrack. No, this audio-visual sensory bombardment calls for something a bit more psychedelic. Like a tray of brownies and a pitcher of Kool-Aid. Turn up the volume, and turn off the lights – not the lava lamp, man! The smoker you drink, the more you're going to get it.

Elvis sightings and secret messages on albums played backwards have never really intrigued me. But when I read about the bizarrely coincidental properties of these two classics I just had to check it out. Floyd and Oz? A strange brew, but a combination with undeniable appeal. Like putting fruit in the yogurt. Ice cream in the root beer. Ice cubes in the hookah.

The sentimental fever was contagious. I mowed the lawn and invited a couple of lunatic friends over. Three remotes in hand, and a comfortable numbness later, we reclined and got ready to get weird. To suggest that we were eager participants in this fantastical experiment is a bit of an understatement. If this had been an "Alice in Wonderland" collaboration we would have tried to climb into the television.

Timing is everything, according to the article I had read. The trick was to start the album at the end of the third roar of the MGM lion. Easy enough, if you're in a lighted room and the men on the chess board aren't calling signals. I was money on the fourth try. (Note: the first roar looks more like a meow – but it counts.)

We found synchronicity almost immediately. In the opening credits. Houston, we are not having a problem. Major Tom, just take your shirt off and relax. We definitely have contact. Pass the brownies, please.

The music hadn't even started yet. But the slow fade-in to a heartbeat while pint-sized credits scroll and thunderheads roll into Kansas put the hook in us early. Then came a nice segue to a full-band sound as the producer's name slid onto the screen in BIG LETTERS. Beam me up, Scottie.

I'm afraid they're going to have to rearrange the history books, because this is Tommy's big brother. Rock-opera in its infancy. Every picture tells a story and every song is a hallucinogenic Cliff's Notes. Did you see that?

When Dorothy leans her head against Toto and closes her eyes, the alarm from "Time" goes off. Wake up, kid! Because here comes wicked Miss Gulch with a terrier-sized picnic basket.

Then there's the tornado sequence. Oh, the tornado sequence. Ohhhhoooo-oohhhoo, ooooohhh-oooooo. I'm not frightened of dying. There's no reason to be frightened.

This is "The Great Gig In the Sky," which synchs nicely first with the terror of the approaching funnel cloud, and then with the surrealistic dream sequence Dorothy pillows into. "The Gig" drifts into an eerie silence when the house lands and Dorothy is crossing the living room towards the front door. The color of "Money" registers splendidly. This sequence is like Hitchcock on two hits of Warhol.

I'm being very sparse with the details here, but you could probably still argue coincidence. Substance-induced dementia. Conspirator's wonderland. Puffs of purple haze on the grassy knoll.

But tell me that "Us And Them" doesn't smack your daddy. Don't even think about the fact that the ensemble cast moves entirely in beat with the music. Forget about the "we're only ordinary men" line as the munchkins come marching up. Smiles, everyone, smiles.

Because when you see who is on screen when Pink sings "Black, black, black." (Clue: Nasty Miss Gulch in full alter-ego regalia.) And then when you see the camera shift and who is in focus when they sing "...blue, blue, blue." (Clue: Dorothy wearing what colored dress? huddled against someone GOOD from the East.) Followed by the line "... and who knows WHICH is WHICH...." You're going to want my brownie recipe.

FSU Break Magazine - September 24, 1997

Book Me, Dano

I don't know about you, but I don't read as often as I used to. Books, that is. I still read a couple of magazines a month, and at least one newspaper a day. But it is a rare occasion when I put down a novel I've just finished. I wonder what happened?

When I was a kid, I used to go after books the way ants goes after sand grains when they're building a mound. Put one down, go get another one. A lot of times I would finish a really good book, then I would start reading it over again. I think I read "Tom Sawyer" nineteen times when I was in third grade. I don't think I've read nineteen books in the past ten years.

Man, I used to love a good book. What did happen? I still buy books. I've got dozens I haven't read. What do I do now with all the time I used to spend reading? Time. Time is the key ingredient, isn't it? That's the easy answer. I just don't have the time anymore.

But that's not really true, and we both know it. The problem is television. I watch too much TV. I get sucked into the old brain mulcher way more than I should. Sports and movies are killing me. I don't even watch the network stuff. I'm a true cable guy. Braves. ESPN. HBO. I just watched "Groundhog Day" six nights in a row. I could have learned ice sculpting in that time.

It seems like I watch a different part of "Full Metal Jacket" about once every two weeks. I'm still trying to figure out what's so great about Kubrick. And I know way too much about Greg Maddux. Love to watch him pitch, but I could have skipped the last five interviews I've seen. What really irritates me is when I watch a good movie on a network station. All those commercials and edited scenes. No more "Dirty Harry" on TNT for me, I swear.

What actually happened was two-pronged: cable and remotes. Cable TV brought us the unending smorgasbord of mind candy. For just a few cents a day you can stay in your armchair and be happy forever. If you have a remote. And who doesn't have a remote anymore? I think I have seven.

Therein lies the problem. Sometimes I pick up a book and start reading, but nothing exciting happens on the first page. What am I supposed to do, walk across the room and get a different book? With remote control in hand, I never have to suffer through a moment of boredom. Surfing for a good channel kind of takes on an excitement of its own.

When I was a kid, we could only get three or four channels on our television. There was no remote. And only one boob tube for the whole family. So, when the parents flipped the dial to Ed Sullivan or Lawrence Welk, it was off to the reading room for me. Sometimes it would take me two or three chapters to get into the book I was reading. But I would suffer and plod on because I could hear the orchestra blazing away in the background. I really don't remember ever not finishing a book that I got two chapters into.

So, I've decided I'm going to start reading books again. I'm going to swivel my chair away from that electronic Cyclops and put a halogen lamp over my shoulder. I'm going to pull out the afghan my mom made me when I went to college and cover my bare feet with it. I'm going to get a globe of red, red wine and put it on the end table next to me and sip at it knowingly when the author makes a subtle point that I cleverly pick up on.

I'm going to take myself back to my childhood where I could escape the madness at a moment's notice by flipping to the bent page corner. I'm going to read myself to sleep. Three or four times a day. I'm going to read the classics and I'm going to read the crap. Dostoyevsky and Grisham. Camus and Sheldon. Bring it all on. Take me to your readers!

This is not going to be easy, I know. The big, dark, silent screen is going to stare me down like a mean dog in a back alley. I don't know who is going to blink first.

The cable box numbers are going to be a luminescent beacon, teasing me from the shadows. Out of pure habit I'll run my fingers over the restless channel buttons of my favorite remote. The theme from SportsCenter will play relentlessly in my head.

There will be no patch to help me through this. No gum to chew away the cravings. It's just going to be me against The Man. I'm going to need something special to get me started. A good – really good – book. A nice fat one to get me past the early stages of withdrawal.

I hope "Tom Sawyer" is still as good as it used to be.

Gadsden County Times – October 2, 1997

The Waiting Game

Some people say that if you have your health, you have everything. It seems to me that this is much truer for sick people than for healthy people. Healthy people can always think of things they don't have. More money. Nicer cars. A house on the beach. So, I don't know if it's true that you have everything if you have your health. But I do know what you have if you are not healthy.

Waiting rooms. Waiting rooms are the medical black holes for the sick, the ailing, the wounded. You don't go to the doctor anymore when you're not well. You go to the waiting room at the doctor's office and stay there until you're better. "Take a number, you're right after Mr. Beetlejuice over there." With all the technological advances and computerized appointments, patients are still loaded into doctors' offices the way refugees were loaded onto shrimp trawlers during the Cuban Flotilla.

I haven't been that healthy lately, so I've been to see doctors a lot. I haven't seen the doctors a lot, but I have had plenty of time to inspect the waiting rooms of several physicians. It is not a pretty story.

On my most recent visit to a family physician, I spent more time in the holding pen than Papillon. The room was an incubator for contagious diseases. Small, warm, and stuffy. I figure it took about fifteen minutes for everyone else in the room to get a good dose of the whooping-lung infection germs I was hacking up. I think with a good black light we could have tracked the flight pattern easily.

To help facilitate the introduction of new diseases into my own system, I leafed through an ancient Sports Illustrated. It was not a magazine, it was a petri dish. I could feel tiny armies of invisible bacteria crawling up my skin.

Then a funny thing happened to me at the one hour and twenty-minute mark of my wait. I wigged out. I lost my feverish cool. I broke the unwritten commandment of all waiting rooms. I returned to the reception desk and complained. You could hear my name sliding down the list even as I approached.

"My appointment was for three o'clock," I wheezed. The Elgin on the wall now read almost four-thirty. Outside, healthy people were hurrying to happy hour to complain about the things they didn't have.

The receptionist looked at me in shock. The room behind me became very still. I had just pulled the mask off the Lone Ranger. I would have cut and run, but I was still on crutches from a recent knee surgery. The knee was stiff from sitting in the orthopedic waiting room for two hours the day before. I froze and stared back like a possum in the headlights.

I never saw the doctor that day. I'm slowly starting to feel better, although I can only detect one lung working when I breathe. I'm using home remedies to treat the pink eye and the sinus infection I picked up on my visit to the doctor's office. I won't be going to that doctor anymore. And I'm not going to my orthopedist tomorrow either. People keep tripping on my bad leg there. I'm not going to see any doctors anymore unless I'm really dying. Unless I'm absolutely terminal. The only doctor I'll ever make an appointment with again is Jack Kervorkian. I hear his waiting room is never crowded.

Gadsden County Times – October 9, 1997

It's Not Just a Job, It's a Fantasy

Here comes America's next big addiction: Fantasy Football. Or Fantasy baseball, or basketball, or even hockey. When it comes to fantasy ownership of sports teams, we can't get enough. This is the new drug Huey Lewis was looking for. No hangovers, no hallucinations. It doesn't cost that much either, unless you value your time. It's cheap, but it ain't free.

Fantasy sports leagues have become an industry. Teams are for sale just about everywhere: in magazines and newspapers, on the internet, even on television. Want to know what it feels like to own more professional teams than Wayne Huizenga? Just contact ESPN's Sportszone. They can put you in the boss's big skybox all year long - in your dreams. You might own Brett Favre, but you're still going to have to catch most of the action from your living room.

Fantasy sports leagues have changed the way we spectate. Armchair quarterbacks have become armchair owners. We don't just watch the games anymore. We scour them for stats. Yards and touchdowns - forget about the final score. We work hard for every inch of turf our players gain. Many an owner has pulled a groin trying to help his wide receiver into the end zone.

We live for the stats. When we ask who scored in the Denver - Dallas game, we really want to know WHO scored. Who had the biscuit in his basket when he crossed the goal line? And how many yards does Emmitt have? How long was Elam's field goal? Did Aikman throw any interceptions?

Information. This is what we need. Which is why sports reporting is undergoing a slow but steady change toward feeding our habit with more numbers. Show me the numbers! Remember when the networks used to show updated scores - just plain old scores? This worked for the office-pool people, or the bartender with the bookie business on the side. But for the fantasy viewer – for the guy with the double-barreled remote in hand – more info was in high demand.

Half-time shows used to be dedicated to quick score updates with a few morsels of individual accomplishments sprinkled in. The bulk of the show featured Terry Bradshaw yelling and panting and making an ass of himself. Now, while Bradshaw continues to make an ass of himself, updated individual numbers run quietly at the bottom of the screen. J. Reed - 158 yds., TD; W. Dunn - 80 yd. rush, 65 rcv. 2-pt. conv. Bradshaw has been relegated to mere background music.

Expect more of the same. And look for newspapers to follow suit. Monday morning box scores are the fantasy junkies' free needle giveaway station. No fantasy owner can hope to contend without memorizing every move every player made on Sunday that was noteworthy enough to warrant a number by his name.

The ultimate goal of fantasy sports is to assemble the most talented team imaginable. You want to stockpile your squad with game-breakers and touchdown-makers. Three hundred yard passers and fifty-yard field goal kickers. Tight ends too valuable as receivers to be used as blockers. Then you want to trade them.

Trade. Oh, what a beautiful word in fantasy sports. Trading is the true reason that fantasy leagues exist. No owner is too busy to talk trade. In the name of trade-talk office work has been neglected. Lawns have not been mowed. Hungry babies have had to feed themselves. Trading is the most sacred and complicated aspect of fantasy sports. Most owners would have less difficulty swapping wives than they would swapping running backs.

Trading is also the true Death Valley for the waking minutes in your day. Songwriter Townes Van Zandt once wrote: "Living's mostly wasting time, and I'll waste my share of mine, but it never feels too good...." He must have penned that while trying to dish Dan Pastorini and

Franco Harris for Joe Theisman and Ahmad Rashad.

It takes a lot of time to pull off the average trade. Nobody wants to be bamboozled. So, after an offer is received, the offeree usually makes ten or twelve phone calls to other owners to see if this would be a dumb move. Then he counteroffers, which starts the process in reverse. This goes on for hours, days, weeks. The deal is only consummated when one owner shmoozes and mentally massages the other owner into submission. A finalized transaction calls for a cigarette and a nap.

Ultimately, being a fantasy owner will give you a new perspective on sports, and on athletes. It will force you to understand why professional teams give wayward players so many extra chances. On draft day, it doesn't really matter to a fantasy owner how many pounds of wonder-herb Bam Morris had stashed in his car. What matters is the 120 yards per game he averaged from scrimmage last year after returning from his drug suspension. And no one cares that Jeff George is the epitome of what we hate about today's athletes. No one cares how many tantrums he throws; they only care about how many touchdowns he might throw. In the true spirit of American sports social values, no fantasy player ever gets too many second chances.

Being a fantasy sports team owner offers the average fan the chance to possess the perfect combination of power and manipulation – what the NFL would get if they crossed Jerry Jones with Bill Parcells. The key to being a fantasy owner is to remember: It's just a fantasy. You do not actually own Carl Pickens. You don't sign his paycheck and you can't call him into your office to see how he likes your new wallpaper. Carl Pickens doesn't even know that you and I exist.

But I'll give you Joey Galloway and Terry Glenn for him right now.

FSU Break Magazine - Oct. 15, 1997

Note: This column was my pitch for a weekly fantasy column. Way before Matthew Berry. Nobody was interested in my fantasy.

A Bedtime Baby Story

My wife and I had a baby fifteen months ago. I remember the labor and delivery like it was yesterday. The whole thing is quite a spectacle. Especially when you consider how really ordinary the birth of a human being is. It's been done a billion times. Maybe more.

So, I knew what to expect this time. I was a veteran. I brought a book and resigned myself to hours of hospital room discomfort. My wife did the same, without the book. They started the labor induction at 7:00 a.m. Very boring. Insert a pill and wait four hours. Repeat.

Let me skip ahead to the fun part. I remember now what I learned fifteen months ago. There is nothing quite as extraordinary as the birth of a human being. Here's what happened.

There I was, just after 5:00 p.m., reading Dilbert and swinging my bad knee, listening to the clicking of renegade cartilage. The Easy-Baby inducing process was moving along swimmingly and labor was looking like nothing more difficult than extracting a misguided pop-tart from the toaster. Then came the nice lady with the knitting needle. (Warning: If you are too short to ride Space Mountain you might want to skip the details forthcoming and meet me later at It's a Small World.)

"I'll just break the water," said the nice lady, "and cross-stitch some booties while I'm in there." So simple, like the jitterbug.

Where is the Dutch boy with his finger in the dike when you need him? The prairie flooded in a nano-second and the townspeople headed for higher ground. The nice lady with the knitting needle looked like an Iowa farmer who forgot to check the Weather Channel. Dilbert was making fun of his boss. I turned the page.

The nice lady had put the knitting needle down now, but there was something strange about her right arm. It seemed to have disappeared up to the right elbow in the general direction of the unborn baby. She turned to the nurse at her side and said, in a calmly comforting voice, "Get Dr. O'Brien, please."

The nurse at her side listened politely. I turned another page.

"NOW!!!" suggested the nice lady with her forearm missing. I suffered a spastic muscle twitch that sent Dilbert flying into the receding floodwaters. The door flew open and important staff people began pole vaulting into the room, screaming and pulling plugs. The intercom was yelling orders and then the woman on the gurney (my wife) waved at me and careened out the door like Curly with Moe and Larry manning the stern.

Somebody dressed me in a paper hat, mask, and gown, and shoved me into a wheelchair. They pushed me into the corridor and left me there to ponder the repetitious harmonies of an early Beach Boys song. A bald leprechaun danced slowly past me and inquired about my knee. A nurse with a head shaped like a computer said, "O.R. 215, Dr. O'Brien." The leprechaun disappeared into swinging doors.

Eight seconds later forty-two people wearing paper hats, masks, and gowns ran through the swinging doors toward me. Must be a party, I thought.

Somebody yelled that Caesar was fine. Somebody else shouted that everybody was a section. They wheeled me through the swinging doors. Two nurses were playing "Toss the Baby" with a radiation-pink ball of flesh. "Here," they sang. "Hold your baby." They handed me the new life; the kid was using blood for Brylcream.

To my left, the leprechaun was poking around inside the baby's old apartment. He had blown up a bloody surgical glove like a balloon and tied it to a spare rib. He told me my knee would be fine. Then he stuffed the balloon into the living room of the baby's old apartment and sewed over it with a No. 7 Mustad fishing hook.

Something wriggled in my hands. The flesh ball had toned down to a factor four sunburn-pink and was looking for something to eat. All I had was half a stick of beef jerky. The kid said I couldn't be serious. A bloody glob of something landed on a tray near my head. The leprechaun was tying a pretty bow of green silk. I glanced at the tray by my head and saw seven bloody globs lined up like jelly doughnuts on a pastry shelf. A baker's half-dozen, I mused. The woman on the gurney (my wife) never said a word.

Then forty-two nurses wheeled me and the kid down to a giant incubator where they fit the baby for a white tuxedo and pointed heat lamps into my eyes. "Eight pounds, eleven ounces," someone announced. The man at the tuxedo counter said, "Big guy. Better give him an XX tiny." My wife slept peacefully through this and dreamed that Ben and Jerry's wanted residual rights to her newly installed feeding station.

The shoes were a little tight, but the kid looked good in tails as he bellied up to the bar thirty minutes later. The clock said six-twenty. "Lucky fella," said my wife, "it's still happy hour. Two for one for new customers."

And thus began the long and storied drinking career of the outlaw-infant who arrived in such stylish fashion. He's popular with the nurses and with the barmaids, who sometimes refer to him as Lucky. A boy-wonder, they say of the kid who nimbly dodged the code-blue bullet known as cord prolapse; who spit in the eye of the hanging judge who tied a true knot in his umbilical cord. He's a handsome gent with a pensive brow and a quick smile for the ladies. And he's a regular now at Mom's All-night Saloon.

Gadsden County Times - October 16, 1997

Note: Bedtime Baby Story is the very true story of the birth of our second son.

The War On Bugs

As a species, humans have an incredibly vast array of feelings about other species. Some we love and protect. Others we seek and destroy. Many we have for dinner. Some species we bring into our homes and treat better than we treat each other. Others sneak uninvited into our homes – we hire trained killers to exterminate them. Hamsters are pets; mice are vermin. Go figure.

Our favorite species might be those that come from the mammal class. People like to go to giant aquariums to see porpoises play. The porpoises would almost certainly rather be playing in the ocean, but if we like a species enough we usually catch a bunch of them and put them in very small confinements. We like porpoises so much that we have been known to boycott tuna companies that killed too many porpoises in their tuna nets. This is probably confusing to the tuna.

We take great pride in protecting whales, too. We used to harpoon them to near extinction, but our mammalian instincts seem to have taken over and saved the whales. For now, anyway. We could always change our minds again. We usually only protect a species until it starts multiplying at its normal biological rate and then starts acting like it owns the earth. If a protected species begins encroaching on our turf, we sharpen up the harpoons pretty quickly.

Maybe that's why the species known as bugs gets no protection at all from people. They are always invading our space. So, we kill them in ever increasing numbers, but they never seem to be in danger of disappearing from the planet. Or from our homes.

We don't bother to keep track of how many bugs there are, or of how many we kill. Deer and alligator populations are counted and closely monitored. But there is no cockroach census. There is no official count of the mosquitoes inhabiting the Apalachicola National Forest. We never even wonder how many ants are roaming the earth. But there must be plenty because we're going after "Them" with a vengeance.

We are specifically targeting fire ants for destruction. And we're getting gruesome in the process. The two latest strategies of eradication involve the help of Mother Nature, albeit a slightly manipulated version. First, we are on the verge of turning loose the Brazilian phorid fly. The phorid fly likes to nest near fire ants. Very near. As in, they like to nest inside the fire ant.

What they do is lay an egg inside the fire ant's body. When the egg develops into the larval stage it wriggles up into the head of the ant which eventually causes the ant head to fall off. Ow. Does Greenpeace know about this?

But wait, there's more. If the phorid fly doesn't lower the head count of fire ants efficiently enough, then we may have to fall back on Beauveria bassiana fungus. Pretty little name for a fungus, yes? But slow death for fire ants. Basically, the fungus attaches to an ant and lives on the protein of the ant's body until the ant has no protein left. Lack of protein of this magnitude causes irreversible rigor mortis in ants.

The obituary for an ant that dies from phorid fly invasion or Beauveria bassiana fungus attachment will read: death of natural causes. Kind of natural anyway. The fungus has been developed by a University of Florida ecologist over the past eleven years and the phorid fly is being imported from Brazil. Just goes to show what lengths we will go to if there is a species we really don't like.

Lots of people are happy to hear this news. But can you imagine the outrage we would feel if the fly or the fungus went to work on Whitetail deer instead of ants? What if a small cloud of flies got in your house and a few days later your dog's head rolled off? Really, it doesn't have to get that drastic before we reverse course on our little nature buddies. All they would have to do is mess with our grapefruits.

See, even as we are considering importing and releasing scads of our new friends, Brazilian phorid flies, we are still swimming in water beds full of malathion we dumped on Mediterranean fruit flies. Good fly, bad fly. Ant head falls off: good fly. Citrus falls off: bad fly. And you thought the tuna were confused?

Clearly, in the war against bugs, the bugs are winning. We've thrown dump trucks of pesticides on them, most of which has ended up in our water supply and on our lettuce. And still the bugs keep coming. So, we'll try a little biological warfare against the bad guys. Heads are going to roll. Better keep an eye on Rover.

Gadsden County Times - October 23, 1997

Homecoming: This Could Be a Real Scream

Homecoming on Halloween. Now that has a nice ring to it. Wasn't this the same theme used in the Jamie Lee Curtis movies where all her friends got hacked into corn beef hash by a masked man-child named Michael Myers? I know, I know, different genre. This Homecoming is about alumni coming to a football game and kids having parties. The movie was about an alumnus coming home and making corn beef hash out of kids having parties. Good thing we have a football game happening.

The Homecoming concept is not that easy to understand. It's not like the football team just got back in town in time for the game. They've been here for at least a week. The students have been here longer than that. And the alumni are not coming home at all. They leave home to come to Homecoming. Just what is it that we are so busy celebrating, anyway?

Basically, Homecoming breaks down to this: The home team plays a patsy – Lee Harvey Oswald University is everyone's favorite – and stomps them like ripe grapes while thousands of cheerleaders, baton twirlers, and mascots whip the packed stadium into a frenzy. Crazed fans can only be sedated by eating several pounds of leathery Polish sausages and washing them down with gallons of smuggled eight-year-old bourbon poured into giant Jimmy Jordan cokes. Students drink themselves into oblivion, helping create warm memories of a special time in their lives. Alumni drink themselves into oblivion reminiscing about the warm memories, and then write checks to the university from their retirement funds. Nobody can remember the score of any Homecoming game that was ever played.

It's not the game that makes Homecoming a big deal. It's the atmosphere. The festivities. It's the parade and the homecoming queen waving at you and pep rallies named after ancient Native American tribal rituals. It's about cancelled classes and floats designed around themes of dubious distinction. It's about the parties. Homecoming is a weekend escape from the usual weekend escapes.

Here's how Florida State's festivities unfold.

Friday, October 31 (Halloween), 1:00 p.m. – Students released from classes. Female undergrads should dress like a teen-aged Jamie Lee, chew huge wads of bubblegum, and stop every thirty feet or so to stare quizzically at tall hedges that someone may be hiding behind. Male students should wear their hair like Donald Pleasance and drive frantically through campus always staying several moves behind anyone that recently busted out of an insane asylum. Alumni should meet at Ken's Tavern and begin the march to oblivion while vainly trying to find where their names were scrawled on the ceiling in a previous moment of oblivion.

**Friday 2:00 p.m. – Homecoming Parade begins on Jefferson St. The theme this year is "Portraits in Progress." Dignitaries of dubious distinction will wave relentlessly at people stopped in the traffic jam created by the parade. Floats will exhibit depictions of the historical progression of FSU. The float detailing the relationship between Burt Reynolds and Loni Anderson was not expected to be ready in time to participate.

Following the parade a street party will take place between Copeland and Gray Streets on Jefferson St. until 6:00. In an effort to prepare fans for the noise volume of Saturday's game, seventy-two strategically located boom boxes will blare forty-seven different kinds of music while the Marching Chiefs pound out the fight song. When the music stops, partyers are encouraged to take a chunk of asphalt with them as a memento of the occasion.

**Friday, 6:00 – 8:00 - No events of festive nature are scheduled for this time slot. You are on your own. Students should avoid going into dark basements to check unusual noises during this time. Alumni should avoid piggybacking to try and fit their names in obscure corners of the ceiling at Ken's. To pass the time more constructively, alumni are encouraged to begin writing checks made out to the university.

**Friday, 8:00 p.m. – Pow-Wow at the Civic Center. Political incorrectness at its finest will happen here. The Marching Chiefs will perform. The Golden Girls will entertain. Cheerleaders will cheer and there will be pep for all. Amidst this gaiety the Homecoming Chief and Princess will be crowned. The trivializing of a proud tribe of Native Americans will be complete when Bobby Bowden, the Seminole football team, and the entire Civic Center audience joins the pepsters in an enthusiastic rendition of the "tomahawk chop."

Following the bloodless carnage, comedian David Spade is scheduled to perform. Spade has co-starred in the movies "Tommy Boy" and "Black Sheep" with fellow Saturday Night alum, Chris Farley. One unconfirmed rumor is that another of Spade's fellow Saturday Nighters will make an unannounced, surprise appearance in Tallahassee. As of this writing, however, the whereabouts of Mike Myers were still a rather troubling mystery.

**Saturday, November 1, 9:00 a.m. – Students should wake up, check to see that all body parts are still attached, take a handful of extra-strength capillary expanders and sleep for two more hours. Alumni should wake up, buy three dozen Bavarian Cream doughnuts and head for the stadium to get those good parking spots. They should also pace themselves on the bloody marys and inspect their investment portfolios for missing parts.

**Sometime later on Saturday – Florida State plays North Carolina State in the Homecoming game. The halftime show will last longer than a nine-inning World Series game and a new record for sausages consumed per capita will be announced. Seventy-five thousand fans will wonder what it's like to watch the game from a skybox, and will stare at the luxury capsules until the glare from the windows injures their retinas. Fans in the skyboxes will watch other games of greater interest on the televisions in the luxury capsules. After the game fans will buy small placards with this inscription on it: FSU - ? N.C. State - ?

FSU Break Magazine - Oct. 29, 1997

Chief Wahoo Meets Pimp Willie

Some people say this year's Florida Marlins v. Cleveland Indians World Series was about mediocre teams. Others say it was about bad television ratings and the best team money could buy. It was a Series with no lasting impressions, they say.

But for me, there was a very lasting impression etched by the 1997 World Series. I just can't forget Chief Wahoo. He grinned me down on every pitch. The lovable logo of the Cleveland Indians put an arrow right through my heart. The red face, the huge white teeth. Chief Wahoo is the indelible image left from an otherwise forgettable event. How did the Cleveland organization ever come up with such a marketing coup?

I don't know what great minds developed the idea of using an entire culture of people as a nickname and a mascot, but the exposure of the World Series is certain to start a trend across the sports world. I can almost see the headlines now. Really, I can. And I can read the stories below them. Here's what they look like:

Marlins, Oilers to Celebrate Ethnic Groups

The Florida Marlins are changing their team name to the Florida Cubans. The new title is in honor of Livan Hernandez, the Cuban-born pitcher who defected to the United States and helped propel the Marlins to the World Series title. The new logo will feature a cartoon caricature of an overweight Cuban man puffing a giant cigar and grinning radiantly through oversized smoke rings.

To help market the new name, the team will introduce fans to a cheer called "The Hot-tempered Latin Man," which will be employed during games as a rally cry. Fans will be exhorted to spew profanities in Cuban and simulate knife fights in the stands.

Front office personnel came up with the name change after admiring the Cleveland Indians team logo during the Series. The Indians use the popular Chief Wahoo – a grinning, red-faced, cartoon-caricature of a Native American – as their team mascot and logo. After researching the origin of the Cleveland nickname, it was discovered that the name "Indians" was selected in 1915 from a newspaper contest to honor Chief Louis Francis Sockalexis, the first Native American to play baseball.

Said one Florida Cuban executive; "You couldn't hate the Cleveland Indians - Chief Wahoo is just so lovable. We want to be lovable too. And we think the 'Hot-tempered

Latin Man' will be more fun than the 'Tomahawk Chop.' We really think we could become the next 'America's Team.'"

"Look," said another Florida Cubans spokesperson, "this change is a tribute to a proud group of people, and it celebrates their heritage. Coming to a Florida Cubans baseball game will be like a small history lesson for kids, and even for some adults."

When asked if the baseball team felt that there was any potential for offending Cuban people with the changes, the spokesperson said, "Hey, political correctness went out with 1995 or '96. Americans love this stuff."

This logic is apparently prevailing, because the Tennessee Oilers have also announced a name change beginning in 1998. The recently transplanted Houston Oilers will play next year's football season as the Tennessee Negroes. The name was selected to celebrate the history of African-Americans in the South.

The Negroes' logo will feature a black man sporting a freshly picked Afro haircut and eating a fried chicken drumstick. "The Afro was strictly a marketing thing, kind of having fun with the whole retro movement. The fried chicken was a no-brainer," said a team representative. The mascot will be affectionately referred to as "Pimp Willie."

The Tennessee spokesperson also discussed the use of

the term "Negroes" as the team nickname. "We basically felt that the Tennessee African-Americans was too long, and not nearly as catchy as the Tennessee Negroes. We thought about calling the team the Tennessee Coloreds, but it seemed too ambiguous. I mean, you have the team colors, you have the color guard, it could have gotten confusing for the fans. We think fans will learn to embrace the 'Negroes' the way fans in Washington, D.C. embrace the Redskins."

A vice-president for the San Francisco Forty-Niners agreed. "We like it," he said. It shows great respect for the history of America. We are seriously considering a name change from the Forty-Niners to the San Francisco Chinamen. We just feel something should be done to recognize the tremendous value of those people to our great land."

An NFL spokesman (he refused to be identified as a spokesperson) stated that the league fully supported this "grass roots movement." "Sports," said the bald, fat guy, "are a microcosm of society. Society in America has always loved the underdog, and who is a bigger underdog than a minority that has been oppressed or stereotyped for many years. By the turn of the century we would like to have teams adopt nicknames that celebrate other proud cultures. We don't want the Irish, the Italians, the Poles – those types – we don't want them left out of this. The New York Godfathers – just think how much fun that would be!"

The spokesman did acknowledge how far professional sports were from attaining the excitement level of collegiate sports. "That thing they do down in Tallahassee with the fake real Indian and the flaming spear. Wow! We can obviously learn a great deal from amateur athletics."

Yes, those are some of the stories I see coming. I can also see the anger the new ethnic nicknames and mascots will create. America is a country that has become super-sensitive to ethnic slights because it has exhibited so many years of extreme insensitivity. So, there will be a lot of anger from a lot of Americans. It's funny how I don't see any of that anger fueled by Chief Wahoo.

Gadsden County Times – October 30, 1997

Dead Babies, and How They Get That Way

If you follow the news these days, you have to wonder if somebody hasn't declared war on babies. Dead toddlers and infants are crowding the headlines an awful lot lately. You kind of get the feeling that something needs to be done. I don't know if the head count is any higher in this particular year than in years past, but it seems like this might be a good time to "just say no" to killing babies.

Just say no. That's the pat answer to most of the perceived ills affecting society today. Drugs: "Just say no." Premarital or teen sex: "Just say no." Drinking and driving – they threw us a real curve ball on this one: "Don't drink and drive." The creative geniuses of these campaigns haven't been carving a lot of new turf, so it's hard to expect that any innovations are coming to thwart the popularity of infanticide.

So, it looks like we're going to have to figure this one out for ourselves. The first thing we have to do is find out who is killing all the babies. We could round up the usual suspects – serial killers, child molesters, etc. – but according to what I'm reading, they are not to blame for most of these deaths. Surprisingly enough, it's a different class of human beings altogether that is leading the league in infant murder. It's the parents.

Sometimes it's a boyfriend or girlfriend of the parent, and sometimes it's a babysitter. But, basically, it is people who are supposed to care for the kid. This is troublesome, because this creates a very large pool of suspects. Maybe the best thing to do is to remove the weapons typically used to kill the children. Round up the usual suspects? Guns, knives, etc.? More trouble, because the weapon of choice is usually the hands.

We're not talking about martial arts experts here. Just good, old-fashioned hands. It doesn't take that much to send tiny babies off to Never-Never Land. Just a good hard slap to the mandible, or a real solid shaking of the child can do the trick. I know, I know, this doesn't really sound like murder. A few years ago it would have sounded like simple discipline. But we didn't know then what we know now.

So, these are the people we have to go after. The ones who take the punishment further – punching, kicking, beating with remote controls, pouring boiling water on genitalia – these people are criminals and need to be dealt with as such.

But the other group – the slappers and the shakers – I

think we can help. We have to help them because we are them. Anybody who has intercourse with a member of the opposite sex is either a parent or a potential parent. Anybody who doesn't think it is possible to lose control so badly while caring for an infant child that slapping or shaking the child might occur is still just a potential parent. Current parents of very small children are just as horrified as anyone when hearing of a child shaken to death. But they would be hard pressed to tell you that they never had the urge to give little Junior a good shake of their own.

The question is, how do we help ourselves? I've got two kids, fifteen months and one month old. The fifteen-month-old child is the most beautiful thing I have ever seen. He likes to stand on the back porch and wave at butterflies and say "bah-bah." When I pick him up from daycare he drops what he's doing as soon as he sees me and runs over anything in his way to get to me. If you ask him for a kiss, he'll plant a nice wet one right on your lips. He melts my heart a thousand times a day.

But there have been times. I am here to testify, there have been moments. There have absolutely been those occasions when I knew that the only solution was to give wonder-boy a good shake or two. Thankfully, I have never given in to the urge. But, strangely, I have a sad empathy for those who have.

The problem for us parents – and for you potential parents – is that we don't know any better. Nobody taught us how to be mothers and fathers. They don't give you an instruction manual when they hand you your baby at the hospital. You made him, you take care of him. And nobody counsels you on how to deal with the frustrating moments that imminently await. The crying jags, the screaming tantrums, the food on the floor, and the food in the hair, and the food in your hair. Then there's the sleep deprivation, the back spasms, and the realization that your life is one endlessly dirty diaper.

Right now we learn about parenting the way we learned about sex twenty years ago – on the streets. We learn from friends, relatives, sitcoms, and bad movies. Or we learn by trial and error. It's the "error" part that is so dangerous. We hear how wonderful children are, and we hear how horrible they can sometimes be. We never hear how to deal with kids when they push us to our limits. If we are going to stop killing our kids, we are going to have to teach ourselves how.

Maybe we can start by borrowing from the philosophy of Alcoholics Anonymous. The first step is to admit that we have a problem. We need to acknowledge that we live in a violent world, a world where we are all overly-familiar with phrases like: "Survival of the fittest;" "Might is right;" and "Only the strong survive." We have to confess that we are an innately violent society, and that we tend to exact physical force on persons weaker and smaller than ourselves.

We need to stand up, one by one, and say things like:

"Hi, my name is Bill, and I can't help it – when my kid throws a tantrum and kicks me in the groin, my first impulse is to smack him one." Someone else is going to say something like: "Hey, my parents slapped me around and I didn't turn out so bad." And someone else is going to suggest that a little physical discipline is what today's kids need.

Then someone that looks just like the rest of us is going to stand up and tell us what it feels like to bury your baby.

Gadsden County Times – November 6, 1997
Tallahassee Democrat – November 9, 1997

War: What is it Good For?

An article I read the other day suggested that we should kill Saddam Hussein at the first viable opportunity. The author – a New York Times columnist – said it should be a head shot. Okay, all in favor, say "Bang!" All opposed, say – well, never mind. I think the "Bangs!" have it.

Saddam is just plain unpopular. Even Nostradamus had it out for the guy. The famous astrologer – according to an interpretive documentary I saw last week – predicted that World War III would be started in the mid to late 1990's by a guy in the Middle East wearing a blue turban. Saddam has been hiding for quite a while, so it's very possible that he's swathed in indigo velvet.

Head-shots? World War III? This is scary stuff. The kind of talk that makes the hair stand up on the back of the stock market's neck. I was thinking of going long on silver certificates and booking a vacation to Canada myself. Instead, I decided to do a little astrologizing of my own.

I headed out on a clear night with a pair of binoculars and a copy of my horoscope from the morning paper. These were the same tools used by Nostradamus when he made his predictions. Amazingly enough, I found that by putting Pluto over my left shoulder, and then lining up a street lamp with the Little Dipper, I could see events that would take place in our near future. I think we're going to be okay.

Here is what I saw. Saddam is wearing turquoise, not blue. And it wasn't World War III Saddam was starting; it was Rambo III. Easy enough to see how the great Nostradamus was fooled. What the super soothsayer didn't know, what he couldn't have guessed back in the 1500's, was that the oil barons would no longer control world events this late in the twentieth century. The power now belongs to network television. Through my binoculars on a cool autumn night, I saw what Paddy Chayefsky already knew.

In my vision I saw Saddam Hussein screaming at a long table of boardroom executives that he was "mad as hell, and he was not going to take it anymore!" The execs ignored him and Saddam pushed a large red button marked "Disaster." Sylvester Stallone appeared on a large movie screen wearing a dirty bandana and a droopy-eyed hatred for foreigners. The board members continued their discussion.

A sharp-tongued, smartly dressed woman was demanding that the networks vote to go to war. Ratings were down, she said. Cable channels were hammering the Big Four. From the disdain in her voice when she said, "Big Four," I could tell she really thought that there were still just three biggies in network TV.

She insisted that a big war was not necessary. "I'm not talking WW III," she said with an exasperated tone. I sighed with relief and took Canada off my list of things to do. Then the fiery woman made a point that sagged the shoulders of the other executives. The World Series was over, she told them. The NFL playoffs are months away. There are no Majors left in the golf year. Nobody watches the NBA until May, and nobody ever watches hockey. The Winter Olympics are – well, they are in the winter. "People," she said flatly, "America needs something to watch."

A few heads bobbed in somber agreement. She outlined the plan for them. The new guy, she said – somebody named Ruppert – would have to go draw the line in the sand this time. The reporters were already in their battle stations, but she wanted them closer to the action. She insisted that the first network to have a news correspondent blow up on air would win an Emmy. To convincingly score a ratings coup over cable channels, somebody was going to have to explode.

The woman warned the others against obvious pandering to audiences, and against overly obsequious behavior. Not too many reporters could be named Storm, she cautioned. And field personnel were to be trained not to remind viewers more than twice a minute how close to the action they were. She wanted no head-ducking during a live interview. The element of surprise would boost viewership, and prevent channel-surfing.

Just when it seemed certain that the networks would vote to start a war in a country on the other side of the world, a man at the end of the table spoke. His head was in a deep shadow, and his voice carried with a booming, otherworldliness resonance. "I have seen the light!" he roared, and the walls vibrated slightly.

The networks, said the shadow, do not need war any more than the economy needs war or any more than big countries need the oil of little countries. America does not watch network television for entertainment, he continued. "They watch it for the COMMERCIALS!" he thundered. "They need to know what sneakers to buy, and they need the world's greatest athletes to tell them."

His voice quieted as he went on. "They need to know what phone companies to choose, and they need popular actors to tell them. They need to know which beer to drink, and they need reptiles to let them know."

A vote was taken then, and it was quickly decided that there would be no war. More Michael, more Candice, more frogs, but no scuds. The meeting was almost adjourned when a diminutive man wearing wire-rimmed glasses reminded the group that Converse footwear stock had dropped almost twenty points since their Dennis Rodman commercials first aired.

"Now there," spoke the man from the shadow, "might be a situation that calls for a head shot.

Gadsden County Times – November 13, 1997

Mistress of the Universe

Kathy Willets is making a fortune. Isn't that great? Kathy is a former prostitute who served six months in jail for running a one-woman bordello from her house a few years ago. Now she is a stripper in nude dance clubs making around half million dollars a year. The law enforcement people in Broward County must be glad they got her off the streets and into the bars where she belongs.

If you draw up a diagram of the two occupations Kathy has employed herself in, it is tough to see where the legal line is actually crossed. For taking off her clothes and having sex with lots of men who paid her lots of money, Kathy was convicted of a crime against the state. Had she had the same sex with the same men for no money, the state would have had to look elsewhere for criminal activity. But, for taking off her clothes and writhing around in a dimly lit saloon where lots of men pay lots of money to ogle and sometimes lay a friendly hand on her, Kathy is getting rich. Legally.

This reminds me of Leon, a bookie that once worked his trade from a bar I tended. He got arrested and spent some time in jail also. Now he's a stockbroker making six figures. Let's draw up this diagram of legality. For allowing customers to wager on a particular team in a sporting event, and for charging a commission only to losers of the wager, Leon got ninety days in the pokey. But for allowing customers to wager on corporations while charging commissions to winners and losers at both the front end and the back end of the venture, Leon gets a nice paycheck and the stamp of approval from the Respectable Society Club.

And what about the customers? I don't think any of Kathy's loyal patrons from her prior job got cuffed, although a few got run out of office, if memory serves. Some of them had their names published and were branded with scarlet J's. Shame, shame, boys.

Now those same bad men can go to the exotic dance establishments and hold their heads up high. They can sit next to lots of respected businessmen and talk mergers and takeovers. A couple of beers and a private dance or two will cost them about the same as an afternoon of consummated desire used to. They can unabashedly ring up the tab on a credit card and take their unrequited passion back to the office knowing that they are law-abiding citizens once again.

Leon's customers were forced into early retirement after his untimely sabbatical. Forced to inspect their frowned-upon hobbies, they took a long look at themselves in the mirror one day. Gambler's Anonymous was knocking at their door. It was no longer socially acceptable to talk point spreads over the Thanksgiving turkey. Something had to be done.

Their lives changed the day Leon got his business cards. They flocked to the phones and placed their money down with renewed vigor. They used to be problem gamblers, now they were wise investors. Overs and unders became longs and shorts. They bought and sold pieces of Americana and gladly gave Leon a sliver of the action every time they ticked a symbol.

As it turned out, some of Kathy's old customers were also some of Leon's old customers. They have been discussing a big business deal every day at The Naked Lunch Café. The rumor is that Kathy Willets is going to incorporate her act and go public, and that Leon has the inside track to buying shares of the initial public offering.

Everyone involved is very happy because the whole thing is so very legal. Kathy is ecstatic because she finally gets to show the whole world her naked torso. Leon is jubilant because he knows he never would have thought of charging double commissions. And the boys are joyous because they have figured out a way to share Kathy's body once again.

Tallahassee Democrat – November 30, 1997

Mr. Bad Example

I think I miss Richard Dawson. You remember Richard Dawson -- the Family Feuder, the man of a million kisses, the guy whose voice rang out with conviction and triumph when he said: "And the survey says...!" If only Rich would shout those lovely words again. I believed it when Richard told me what the survey said. Never had a doubt. But I see the results of all the latest surveys and I wonder who in the stalag came up with these answers.

Take Latrell Sprewell. I know what you're saying – please take him – right? And so they did. They took him for a year, suspended. And they took him for the remaining year of his contract - twenty-four million beanie babies. Now that's a fine. Maybe this is fair and maybe it isn't. The polls all say the public fully supports the decision. But I would be a lot more comfortable with the outcome if Richard Dawson would just bring the old Family Feud format to the sports world. Then I think America could rest a lot easier after hearing what the penalties and fines for obnoxious behavior amount to.

Here's how the procedure would work. Richard Dawson would appear on ESPN whenever an athlete committed a heinous act worthy of national attention. Richard would describe the bad behavior by posing it in the form of a question, and would have free license to add colorful characteristics and details that might seem pertinent to the outcome. It's the "free license" part that I think will be most helpful in easing any angst America might be having over the disparate penalties handed out when athletes do bad things. Let me illustrate for you by using some previously committed heinocities.

Let's start with Baltimore Oriole second baseman Roberto Alomar.

Richard Dawson: "What is the proper punishment when an all-star caliber baseball player spits in an umpire's face while being restrained by several players and coaches and then impugns the umpire's integrity by blaming the ump's lousy attitude and poor calls on the recent death of the umpire's young son?

"Survey Saaays! Allow Alomar to play in the highly popular, strong Neilsen-rated playoff games next week, but be a man and take a suspension next year in the first few meaningless games which will be played in icy conditions that are not really conducive to producing the all-star stats that make us love you."

See how much better you feel when Richard explains the results. Okay, let's do Lawrence Philips. I hear the people in Miami are excited to have him.

Richard Dawson: "How can we adequately sanction a collegiate athlete who plays with one of the most respected football programs in the country if the player drags his girlfriend down three flights of stairs – wow, three flights, he must have had to stop and rest once or twice – by the hair?

"Survey saaays! Sorry, Lawrence, you'll have to sit out the rest of the regular season while your teammates pound foes of high school equivalent ability and then you have to play in the National Championship game on short notice and be vindicated by your well-respected coach so that you may be drafted as low as sixth overall in the following NFL draft."

Amazing, isn't it? It almost seems like there were real consequences for Philips when Richard explains it. All right, here's a good one – Charles Barkley.

Richard Dawson: "What should the NBA do if Sir Charles throws a man through – ha, ha, oh, Charles, you didn't – a plate glass window and then shucks off a police officer in order to stand over the man and taunt him by saying things like 'I hope you die of a rare slow stomach cancer caused by enzymatic secretions released only from glass broken by a physical force of at least seven hundred pounds per square inch' – Charles, you do it with such flair (throws a smooch to the cameras for Barkley) – and then in repeated interviews is quoted as saying he hopes the man dies and warns America not to (expletively!) mess with Sir Charles?

"Survey saaays! Charles, we love you, man! You have our full support in your quest to be elected governor of sweet home Alabama. Grab a rebound for us tonight, Round Mound!"

Enough said. Everyone knows that foreign ambassadors and Charles Barkley have complete diplomatic immunity. Now let's visit with the Latrell Sprewell survey.

Richard Dawson: "What is the appropriate sentence, ah, suspension, I mean, for an extremely talented but mostly unknown all-star who has committed the following atrocities this season: Was seen laughing at a joke on the sidelines during a loss and refused to tell the coach the punchline; wore his hair in braided cornrows (Richard shakes his head in resignation); was late to practice and argued with the coach who has a long history of being the arguer, not the arguee; and finally, attacked the coach with fists and choked him – do we have a picture of the bloodied coach? No blood? No visible bruise? Okay, moving on. Came back a few minutes later and attacked the coach again, and this time threatened to kill him – whoa!

"And the survey saaays! Bye, bye, Mr. Sprewell. How do you pronounce that last name, anyway? Never mind, Mr. Poor Role Model. Mr. Bad Example. Your statistics are no longer valuable to us. Maybe you should get a haircut before you become a statistic, if you know what I mean. Check back in a year, and bring some kneepads, punk.

(Richard somberly faces the camera again.) "People, sometimes our heroes cross the line. And sometimes, Latrell, we have to make them pay."

December 12, 1997

Landmines for Loyalty

Here's a confession of sorts. When I was a kid attending public school, I never said the Pledge of Allegiance. When I was very young I was probably just too lazy, or too busy trying to fire a spit-wad at an unsuspecting neighbor. But as I got older, I started to question the daily recital of loyalty to country. Why, I wondered, did you have to pledge your allegiance every day? Wasn't once enough?

There was always something about the Pledge of Allegiance that made me uneasy. Maybe it was putting my hand over my heart during the recitation. Was my loyalty more assured this way? And what exactly was expected of me if I did participate in the unending ritual? Were the flag and the republic for which it stood promising me something in return?

After graduating from high school, the Pledge disappeared from my life. Apparently, I was in. As a full-fledged member of the Good Guys I would not necessarily ever have to say the words that I had never actually bothered saying again. But my uneasiness with blind-faith patriotism was not over yet.

"The United States is the greatest country on earth." This statement became a popular post-Pledge mantra laid down more frequently than linoleum. I have heard it at dinner parties and cocktail parties, on golf courses and at company picnics. Politicians say it and construction workers say it. It is a very safe and strong statement to make because it is not likely to elicit an argument from people who grew up pledging their allegiance to this country every school day of their lives.

Predictably enough, I am not that comfortable in the company of such a statement. Patriotic hyperbole should be reserved for young country music performers trying to make a name for themselves. Still, I never knew for certain before that the United States was not the greatest country on earth. My suspicions were certainly aroused by the assassinations of the Kennedys, King, and X in the sixties. Vietnam, Nixon, and Kent State did little to allay the doubts. Race riots, the reinstatement of capital punishment, and the backlash against affirmative action have been steady fuel for uncertainty.

But I never knew for sure that we were not top dog until we refused to sign the Landmine Ban Treaty recently adopted by one hundred and twenty-one other countries worldwide. Based on this news, I would say this country ranks no higher than 122nd in global greatness.

Let the crossfire begin. Tell me how wonderful it is that we live in a free land – so free that I can say what I am saying without fear of government reprisals that would be immediate if I lived in China. China bad, U.S. good. Tell me how lucky we are that our country does not suffer the poverty and separatism evinced by the people in India every day. Remind me of the evils of communism and how that misguided philosophy has left Russia in a state of moral and physical disrepair. Tell me about these very countries that we have long insisted we were better than. These are the same countries that joined the United States in refusing to sign the treaty. Also not signing: Iraq, Iran, Vietnam, and Libya. Let's party!

The United States refused to sign an agreement ending the use of landmines? Am I missing something here? We are the Good Guys, aren't we?

Granted, I do not know the international politics that are driving the decisions of the countries that have not signed the treaty. I don't think I need to know. Suffice it to say that third-world civilians are being blown to the glue factory while participating in such ominous exercises as farming, or walking to school. The U.S. policy, I believe, is to use land mines to keep the peace. It must be working, because farmers and schoolkids in Angola have not recently threatened U.S. shores.

According to what I read in the free press of America, this country is most concerned about keeping in place the thousands of land mines separating North and South

Korea. This area is known as the demilitarized zone. Good oxymorons are not usually so easy to spot.

The concern is that without armies of hidden explosive devices in the soil, lots of BAD Koreans – also known as communists – could creep across the DMZ and overpower the GOOD Koreans who supply a lot of the cheap labor needed by American manufacturers. Also at risk are 37,000 U.S. soldiers who are protecting the GOOD Koreans.

The presence of the soldiers in Korea is necessary because without it, communism would rule the world and threaten the freedom of my press. See the Soviet Union, Cuba, and China for documented evidence that the failure of communism is predicated on U.S. military presence in the offending country.

Maybe we are the greatest country on earth. So far, there have been no reports of any land mines planted by foreign nations in United States soil. We are planters, not plantees. This is such good news that I think I'll hoe the garden tomorrow and walk my kids to kindergarten. When I get back, I am going to put my hand on my heart and say the Pledge of Allegiance very loudly.

December 16, 1997

Oh, Not a Pair?

When I first saw the story about the au pair murder trial, I thought there would be a problem getting a conviction. I figured one of them would blame the other one and both would walk. It was a couple of weeks before I realized that the au pair was only one person. Admittedly, I did not read many of the stories about the case. I mostly kept a sharp eye on the headlines and skimmed through the paper to Doonesbury. But I would wager that not a single newspaper defined the term "au pair" for its readers when the story broke.

This is what newspapers do. They just tell the story, they don't explain it. For example, does anybody know why the Irish Republican Army puts bombs in train stations every few weeks in England? If you read the newspaper, you have seen these headlines a thousand times. But have you ever seen an explanation for the mayhem? As nearly as I can understand from reading the newspaper every day for the past twenty years, the IRA wants the English out of Ireland.

But I don't know why England is in Ireland or why it insists on staying. England just gave Hong Kong back to China. They let Barbados, India, and the Bahamas rule themselves. What is so precious in Ireland that they continue to subject their citizens to random mutilation?

I don't know what the hell is going on in the Middle East either. In twenty years of daily newspapers I could probably count on one hand the number of times that the front page did not carry a story about unrest in the Middle East. But I still can't figure out why children throw rocks at armed soldiers who really don't seem to have a problem spraying the crowd with a little gunfire. Are they fighting over land or religion over there? Do they expect a winner to be announced sometime soon?

Maybe I'm not the only one who does not understand these things. Maybe nobody understands them, and that's why nobody tries to explain them. Perhaps the newspaper people only know that it is their job to put these particular stories on the cover of as many newspapers as possible. That would help explain why two dead in Israel get front page coverage, while two thousand dead in Somalia get a paragraph on page thirteen next to a story about a two-headed cow.

But why does a drought caused by El Nino that results in a crop failure on a Venezuelan farm get the front page, while a typhoon that destroys an island in the Philippines gets a page number that Paul Harvey never reaches? Michael Jordan's salary gets more print than the volcano that is threatening to turn Montserrat into the world's biggest lava lamp.

It is difficult to figure out if newspapers are giving us what we want, or if they are giving us what we need. The au pair story seems to fall in the "what we want" category. Something there caught our fascination and the press fed us like pigeons at the park. They didn't give us what we need though, because we still don't know what au pair actually means.

I'm not sure we want any more headline stories about the Middle East or the IRA. But we must need them, because they are as endlessly prevalent as those pigeons in the park. It's clear that the papers think we "need" to hear about all the bloodshed, but that they don't think we "want" to know the reason for it.

We certainly don't need to know Michael Jordan's salary. But we would want to know if he was spending any of it to help out disaster-stricken islanders around the world.

Wouldn't it be strange if people only wanted to know what they needed to know, and if that was all the newspaper printed? I don't think that would leave much for the reporters to do. We wouldn't have a clue what happened yesterday near the Syrian border. Not knowing wouldn't change a thing we do in our regular day, because knowing what happened never changed a thing we did.

Newspapers can report whatever news they desire to us. They can entice us to read a story we have no real interest in just by using GIANT HEADLINES. Let's hope they never depart too far from reporting the news we want to know because we need to know. Because in the morning, I guarantee you, Montserrat citizens really don't need to read any stories other than the one below this headline: "Volcano to Erupt Today!"

Tallahassee Democrat – January 4, 1998

Best of the Tops:
The Far Side of 1997

Looking at a calendar is not the best way to tell that the year is coming to a close. If you are interested in what kind of shape Cindy Crawford or Tyra Banks is in, then looking at a calendar is the best thing to do. But the best indication that 1997 is slowly nodding off is the deluge of "Best of" and "Top Stories" features that the media drowns us in. A calendar year is not officially logged into the history books until someone reminds us of the significant events that occurred that should have affected our lives in some way.

If this is my duty, then so be it. I decided to scour my personal resource archives for events that were particularly newsworthy in 1997. I found my files clogged with stuff that is just too serious to be considered here. I believe it is the strange, unusual, and bizarre stories that set one year apart from others. To properly complete the task, I was forced to pour a goblet of champagne and put a party hat on. A magnum of glitter-laced bubbly later, I finished culling the best of the best. Here then, in no particular order, are the top five news events of 1997.

1. Bear With Me: In late spring or early summer, someone reported that a bear was swimming in the Gulf of Mexico. The Game and Freshwater Commission sent a boat out to catch the bear. With a net. Footage of the attempted capture has not yet aired on "America's Funniest Home Videos," but bears everywhere are said to still be laughing. The bear in question eluded the nets and was last seen backstroking towards Cedar Key. The Game Commission has vowed not to be foiled next time. Acting on a hunch after viewing a "National Geographic" special, the Commission now plans to troll for swimming bears with whole salmon.

2. Squirrelly Behavior: A man in Edgewater was charged with a third-degree felony for shooting a squirrel with an arrow. The squirrel was eating the man's tomatoes and papayas. There are several ways to go with this, I think. First, animal rights aside, you really do have to say – nice shot, man.

Second, I think the guy should have thanked the squirrel for eating his papayas instead of ventilating his spleen. I've tasted papaya, and nothing short of an arrow pointed at me could persuade me to try another slice.

Third, the felony charge seems a bit steep. I mean, I know a guy – and I won't use my real name here – who had a serious squirrel problem. They were going through his bird food the way Shaq goes through a roll of toilet paper after a bad burrito. So, the guy doused the sunflower seeds with the hottest pepper powder on the market. Capsicum. Red dust that promised to smoke the little thieves like Tiparillos. Charges could have been filed here also. I think the worst they could get would be Attempted Squirrel Battery though, because the pepper sauce did not work. The squirrels winked away a tear or two, disappeared, then showed up minutes later with margaritas and ate until their bellies distended.

Tough little rodents, ain't they? The squirrel with the arrow through it got away.

3 & 4. Fresh Garbage meets the Space Station: Two stories in the same paper, same day. They seem unrelated, but bear with me (again). Story one says that the landfills in New York City are racing quickly towards the past tense. "Landfull" could soon be a word. So, the Big Apple is in the export business when it comes to leftovers. The problem is that importers are getting harder to find. What do you do with thirteen tons of fresh refuse a day when the disposal gets clogged?

See story number two. Page ten. An idea begins to emerge. Because high over Gotham City, scientists have photographed a black hole. Black holes are invisible, which makes it difficult to tell when the film is actually developed. But this one sits in the center of our galaxy and sucks stars and gas clouds into the vortex, which swirls around at about a million miles per hour. This sounds even stronger than the F-5 tornado that had Bill Paxton and Helen Hunt flapping horizontally in last year's blockbuster comedy. This is a serious suck zone. Nothing like the one I was in when I paid seven bucks to see "Twister." When a star gets Hoovered up by the black hole, it disappears. Gone.

Are you with me so far? We've got all that garbage that's crowding out the people. And we have all that suction in space. I showed the two articles to the sanitation engineer working my street one day. He read them and looked at me thoughtfully. "We put a man on the moon, didn't we?" he asked.

"And we built the Alaskan Pipeline," I offered.

He looked up at where he imagined the invisible black hole was vacuuming away and said, "Are you thinking what I'm thinking?"

5. Big Blues: The great Kasparov lost a chess match to a computer chip. That hurt. The human ego does not take lightly such slights from the technology it designs.

But maybe this was really good news. Maybe we could use this defeat to redirect our angers and fears and jealousies towards machines instead of each other. Maybe we could start shooting the other guy's car instead of the other guy. We could beat up the microwave instead of the wife. Throw the remote out the window instead of the kid.

We could trash a lot of machines and be a lot healthier for it. And it would be good for business, too. Production lines would really start humming. Steven King never thought of it going this way.

Well, those are the news events that pushed the needle the highest on my Bizarre Meter. 1997, I miss you already. Happy New Year, everyone. I need to spank my keyboard now.

January 7, 1998

Will the Real President Please Stand Up?

So, who is this joker, Richard Seed? He says he is going to start cloning humans. Is that his real name, or did he change it to reflect his secret desire to plant an embryo in every living womb? Was he a porn star before becoming a scientist? I don't know about you, but I can't seem to take this dude too seriously. I'll start believing when a bunch of little Seedlets start showing up.

What I want to know is why President Clinton is all shook up by Seed's proposal? Clinton stated in his weekly radio address that he found the notion of human cloning to be "profoundly troubling." Correct me if I'm wrong, but if something is profoundly troubling you, wouldn't that something pretty much consume your waking moments? And I don't think you can be profoundly troubled by more than one thing at a time. That means that right now Saddam Hussein's biological warfare arsenal comes in at least a distant second on the presidential worry-meter.

Where does this leave nuclear testing, global warming,

and Mad Cow disease?

Personally, I think the Big Cheese might be losing his marbles. Listen to some other comments he made on the radio broadcast. "...I believe that human cloning raises deep concerns given our cherished concepts of faith and humanity." And he said the process was "untested and unsafe and morally unacceptable."

I'm afraid he lost me at the "cherished concepts" part. I'm not sure I ever had any of those. But if I did, would they be violated by the idea of a cloned human? I really can't imagine that my cherished concepts could be any more compromised by a human "Dolly" than they could be by a fertility-drug-induced birth of septuplets.

In this modern world we have sperm banks, in-vitro fertilization, and genetic testing. And we have abortion clinics. Could the President be a little more clear on what exactly "our cherished concepts of faith and humanity" are? Are his concepts supposed to be similar to mine? Could he also please point out the line where advancing medical capabilities become "morally unacceptable?"

The thing is, when you start using phrases like "morally unacceptable," you create an irreversible conundrum of conflicting philosophies. For example, some people think the death penalty is okay, but don't believe abortion should be legal. Taking a life in its second trimester is morally unacceptable for these folks, but taking the same life in its ninetieth trimester can – according to columnist

George Will – satisfy a "wholesome desire for vengeance" under the right circumstances. (If George finds the death penalty wholesome, I don't want to know what family hour is like around his house.)

Other people find the death penalty morally unacceptable, but believe in a woman's right to abort a fetus she is carrying. Mass murderers get to breathe the light of day under this philosophy, while developing embryos play the lottery.

Now, let's talk again about "our" cherished concepts of faith and humanity. I may be going out on a limb here, but I don't think we are all on the same team out here. I don't think we are supposed to be. You have your cherished concepts and I'll have mine. You donate your sperm and I'll cryogenically freeze my head. One of us might live forever. You get a pig liver transplant and I'll get myself cloned. While I'm discovering my inner child you can have a staring contest with a ham sandwich.

But please, Mr. President, don't tell me you find any of this profoundly troubling. Be troubled by postal employee rampages, or even by postal rate increases. Find the genocidal massacres of helpless villages to be morally unacceptable. I'll be with you on all of these. We can be part-time teammates. But get off Richard Seed's back.

If you're going to start spewing presidential hyperbole every time some mad doctor who is unapproved by the FDA claims he can build Frankenstein from a nip of human tissue, people are going to be put off. They are not going to vote for you anymore. They'll start looking for someone else.

They will want someone a lot like you, though. Someone with the reassuring leadership style you possess. Someone who can finesse his way out of any kind of ethical jam. They will want someone who looks good, speaks well, and is obviously intelligent. Someone just like you, but not you. Where do you think they can find a guy like that?

January 13, 1998

Golf: A Good Game Spoiled

Man, I love the game of golf. It could possibly be the greatest game ever invented. If you have ever teed up a ball and spanked it into orbit, and watched it gut the fairway and roll farther than you thought possible for an object propelled by your own meager talents, then you might agree with me. Words could never properly convey the inner euphoria that one celebrates at such a moment. Few sports offer as generous an interval of self-admiration as golf does after a good shot.

On the other hand, golf can leave you feeling a little dirty, also. Not from sweat, or mud, or from sand blasts into the wind. Golf is more likely to dirty your conscience. Golf has long been an elitist sport, reserved for wealthy white males. These merry gents have a storied history of shushing the crowd while they play, and of preventing women, blacks, and other persons of ethnic or religious disfavor from joining them. "Members Only" has often really meant "Exclusively for guys just like us."

Many people thought the barriers were starting to tumble after Tiger Woods burst onto the scene. Then came the news that Tiger practiced between events at a club that did not allow women on the grounds. The Master's victory by a player of African-American descent could suddenly be summed up by paraphrasing one of the great quotes in United States history: One small step for man – no steps at all for women.

It is really no surprise then, that the game of golf is refusing Casey Martin's request to use a golf cart on the PGA tour. Casey Martin has a birth defect – a circulatory disorder - that makes walking difficult and painful. But he can play golf at a level very near, if not equal to, other members of the PGA tour. He just needs a ride to keep up. The boys who run the show don't care. And neither do most of the players on the tour who have been interviewed.

The PGA officials and the PGA tour players who have spoken out against allowing Casey Martin the use of a golf cart are an embarrassment to the sport. The fellas are outdoing themselves. They are making Fuzzy Zoeller and Ben Wright look like humanitarian crusaders.

The issue is simple, according to the men who make the rules. No golf carts are allowed because using one would be an unfair advantage. The rulebook probably never considered that persons born with two good legs inherently have an unfair advantage over a person born with only one good leg. Undoubtedly, the rules were written by a bunch of guys with – you guessed it – two good legs.

And there you have the process that makes the game of golf so easy to dislike. The guys at the country club who wrote the rules excluding blacks were almost certainly not men of color. Probably no wives were on the committee that prohibited women from playing. Seems like there ought to be a law against this.

Because you can bet that if Casey's disorder – Klippel Trenaunay Weber Syndrome – was extremely common, there would be no issue here. If lots of the rich, stately gents of the game limped around like Ratso Rizzo on a cold winter day, you can be sure there would be no rule against golf carts as part of the equipment. Casey's problem is that there just are not enough of his kind around the clubhouse.

It is interesting to note that if Casey Martin's disability were his eyesight instead of his leg, he would not need to petition for a rule change. If Casey was blind he would need somebody to help him pick out the correct golf club to hit. Somebody would have to tell him how far and what direction he needed to hit the ball. Someone would have to line him up over his putts and detail the speed of the green and any breaks it might have.

Yes, Casey could have someone do all these things because all professional golfers have someone do these things. They call them caddies. Caddies are allowed on all PGA tour events.

Who do you think wrote that rule? There are several choices here. It could have been some lazy men who just wanted someone to schlep their clubs. It could have been penned by stupid men who never could figure out the nuance of the game. Or it could have been inspired by the plight of a tournament golfer or two who were afflicted with a debilitating disability in the days before golf carts were born.

The game of golf is nothing if not a labyrinth of rules. Some seem economically logical, while others seem purposefully arcane. There is simply no reason that the rule against golf carts could not be abolished, or amended satisfactorily. I believe a PGA rules committee exists for situations just like this.

Instead, the PGA has delivered golf another white-collar black eye. A little pop on the noggin to remind everyone of the safety of the status quo in this country-club-civilized sport. It may not look good to a world with a heartbeat, but it protects the integrity.

Man, I hate the game of golf sometimes.

Tallahassee Democrat – January 21, 1998

The Lewinsky Address

Okay, he's guilty. Let's get that out of the way first. Bill Clinton undoubtedly seduced young Monica Lewinsky and showed her exactly what happens when the President gets excited about his election. (That's "election." With an "l.") Now let's figure out why we're so fascinated by this. It seems to me that the presidential organ we should be most concerned about is the brain. The big head is the one that can start a war - the evil miniature can only engage in the occasional swordfight. But we never give much thought to what the President's brain is up to.

A small misfire in the gray matter and we could lose jobs, money, security, or freedom. The wayward whereabouts of the presidential penis, on the other hand, have no real impact on our daily lives. Gasoline prices don't go up and interest rates are unaffected by reports of strange noises coming from the broom closet of the oval office. Still, the American public's interest is clearly more titillated by the adventures of Bill's willy than they are by the advent of actual missiles pointing towards Iraq in a state of arousal.

This is where we are in 1998. We could go to war today and not find out about it until after it is over. And we just might if the story in yesterday's newspaper on page four is true. James Carville declared war on Republicans over the Lewinsky mess and that was reported on page two. But a report on an imminent military strike by the United States on Iraq was relegated to page four. If Monica Lewinsky decides to hold a press conference today, we will have to subscribe to the Baghdad Times to find out what happened in Desert Storm II.

We clearly need to redivert our attention here. I'm not suggesting that we need to forget all about the hyperactivity of the President's genitalia. But maybe we could just return the full salute and move on to more important issues. At least we could attempt to give world issues equal time. I could live with that.

The speechwriters could help. They could begin with the State of the Union address the President is about to deliver. Start him off with something like, "Four scores and seven affairs ago, I took this office with a commitment to the American people – a real commitment, not like the thing I have with my wife." This will be known historically as "The Lewinsky Address."

Then he could talk about lowering taxes or improving race relations. Now this is the kind of speech we would actually listen to. The President could sprinkle it with sexual innuendo and recount the unusual positions he was in when he formed his policies. Like this:

"Just last week Ms. Lewinsky and I, along with a fellow staff member, were hiding in a storage closet when I realized the importance of removing the marriage penalty from the federal income tax regulations. I knew right then that I would to continue to push and pull Congress until this provision is repealed."

I think viewer ratings would go way up. The public would finally tune in to what the President had to say. Reporters could help also. Questions to the President could be phrased to include all recent White House developments. Like this:

Sam Donaldson: "Mr. President, is it true that you appointed two new federal judges today while you were engaged in non-adulterous sex with a young intern?"
President Clinton: "Why, yes, Sam, that would be accurate. There is just such a dire need to fill these positions with capable people who know the rules."

Now we're getting somewhere. This way our prurient curiosity gets satisfied while the business of the world is efficiently reported. The war can move back to the front page where it belongs. From now on sex scandals and international issues can share the same headline. Like this: "Clinton Orders Two Missile Attacks – One of Them on Iraq."

January 27, 1998

(Note: To my knowledge, this column was never published, although it was submitted to both the Gadsden County Times and the Tallahassee Democrat. I was not informed of the non-publication until I found out by asking where the hell my column was. Too risqué was the suggested reason for declining to print. Those were just more delicate times I guess.)

The Dead of Winter

Any man's death diminishes me, because I am involved in mankind.

- John Donne

I had my wife's cat put to sleep this morning. If everything went according to plan, Dash should be dead by now. She should have gotten a lethal injection and been bagged off to the crematorium. I never liked Dash much. Dash never liked me at all. In fact, Dash never cared for any person besides my wife. Dash, the cat, never had anything more than a hiss or a spit for any other human that dared get close.

But my wife cried when she handed me Dash in the cat carrier this morning. She is probably not done crying yet. Dash was fifteen years old, which in cat years is way older than Lorne Greene. And Dash had a tumor that was open and growing larger. Dash had not eaten food in at least a week. Dash's time had clearly come. The only humane thing to do was to take Dash to the cat-Kervorkian. Still, there are all those tears.

And then a funny thing happened when I was at the vet. The girl behind the counter said, "I'm sorry about your cat." I looked around, confused momentarily, to see if my wife was behind me. I was alone.

No, really, I wanted to say. I hate this cat. Been waiting for this day for years. But I didn't say any of that. I just kind of looked at this girl who was so concerned about "my" cat, and I realized that the bells were about to toll. It occurred to me then that it really did not matter who was going to the sleep eternal, the bells really do toll for thee. And thee was me. And I found myself getting a little misty-eyed.

***

If you have to eventually come home from your weekend getaway, and if the drive has to take ninety minutes, then the road back from St. George Island to Tallahassee is not a bad stretch of highway to have to traverse. A little water, a little country. Nothing spectacular, just quietly scenic in a casual kind of way. Very nice on sunny Sunday morning, even in the dead of winter.

But the view can get ugly quickly. Like yesterday when we came upon a possum in the early stages of road kill. The possum was circling itself slowly in the center of the highway. It had a dazed, but still angry look on its face, with teeth bared in a scowl. But the legs wobbled uncertainly, and a rivulet of blood ran between eyes that revealed far more fear than menace.

Cars heading in both directions slowed as they passed the animal, and veered slightly in their own uncertainty before accelerating purposefully away. Our car did the same, despite my every inclination to stop and help in some way. I just don't do wounded possums well. Or any other injured, semi-crazed, wild critters. I'm just a sissy city-boy.

If everything went according to plan, that possum was dead before I turned into our driveway. I saw a couple of buzzards softly circling the highway minutes after we passed the possum, and I tipped an imaginary hat to the horrors of the food chain.

We had a very good time on St. George, but I keep seeing that bloody, frightened face, and I hear the bells toll every time I do.

***

If everything goes according to plan, Karla Faye Tucker will be dead by the time you read this. Texas don't play around. Karla Faye got prettied up, and Karla Faye got God, but Karla Faye didn't get clemency. And, of course, she shouldn't get clemency for the aforementioned reasons. Religion and good looks have nothing to do with the law. Says so right in the constitution.

I can't think of a worse reason to spare a person's life than that person's belated claim to Christian conversion. Karla Faye would never have made a single front page if she had become a devout Buddhist. But I can't think of a better reason either.

There is nothing to be gained by the involuntary and unnecessary extinction of another life.

There is no sympathy here for pick-ax murderesses. None for any of the death row population. Every sympathy is for her victims, and her cellmates' victims, and for all of their families. But the bells are still going to toll when Karla Faye goes to the sleep eternal. And the bells will not toll any less for the murderers than they did for the victims.

The bells, as always, will toll for thee. And thee, as always, is we.

February 3, 1998

Tied to the Whipping Post

I received an e-mail this morning from a friend of mine that directed me to open an internet site that was highlighted in the text. I'm just a lemming with a java buzz in the A.M., so I double clicked and was treated to a photograph of a large exotic bird perched firmly on the aroused genitalia of an otherwise unidentified man. Very nice. My pop tart wasn't tasting that good anyway.

But it was my next e-mail that was really shocking. It seems my friend had distributed the same directive to several other people, including his father. Dad did not see the humor. Dad, in short order, expressed his deepest disappointment that his own offspring had served up this rude offering. In the spirit of this techno-modern age, I would say dad gave son a serious E-spanking. In public.

Shocking! My friend is an adult man with a wife and a kid. He's an attorney in a respected law firm. He's the commissioner of my Fantasy Football league! But dad went after him with wet-tipped rhetoric the way

Singapore goes after graffiti artists. Kind of makes your cheeks twitch, doesn't it?

Well, here's what I have to say to the old man: Nice work! Can I get a little E-pplause out there? Come on, everyone, let's give dad a standing "E." Take a bow, pop.

I have one request of my pal's father, though. Can we get the rest of the fathers out there to join you? And how about the moms? How about a little maternal scolding to stir into my coffee?

Let's face it, it's a rude, rude world we live in. Maybe the only hope we have to remain civilized is for the parental units to play a larger role. Maybe it is time we start getting public statements from the parents of all the people who make a living being rude. Where do we start?

I would start with ESPN. Yeah, the sports network. I tuned in to the ESPY awards last night expecting a little sport mixed with a little humor, which is the trademark of the station. Irreverence is generally a good thing for sports. But ESPN substituted bad taste for mirth. They trotted out a Harry Caray impersonator who groveled for giggles by extolling the heroics of John Elway, and then while the camera focused in on Elway, suggested that John use some of his riches to fix his teeth.

Is there a dad in the building? Your son, the impersonator, just embarrassed your entire lineage.

Who else makes the All-Rude team? I would say that the morning talk show personalities that have infected the frequencies of seemingly every radio station available could use a word from the ancestry. It's bad enough that the shock-jocks have denied me the pleasure of hearing a good tune on the way to work. But listening to their lowest denominator prattle is like being caught in a drive-by crossfire of ill-bred manners.

Nobody has ever accused me of being genteel. In fact, members of my listening audience have occasionally left the room in response to my lack of decorum. The e-mail with the questionable content did not offend me in the slightest. But I will say this. I don't remember ever getting an e-mail from that same friend that just said, "hello, how's it going?" He never sends a cute anecdote about his child. I have no idea what is happening in my buddy's life, but I receive a steady sampling of lewd forwards that remind me of our acquaintance.

Maybe my friend has become so immersed in the world of common rudeness that we live in that he didn't realize someone might be offended by his otherwise generous dispersion of the photo. I know I didn't think twice about it until I read the publicly displayed, cyber-sent lip lashing from his dad.

So maybe ESPN and the morning radio shows need a phone call from the moms and dads too. Maybe the whole world needs a little parental commentary on the antics of the offspring. It could be a good thing to hear from the folks when we're not making them proud.

That being said, I just want to add this. I hope my own mom and dad read or listen to my comments here. I hope I have always made them nothing but proud and continue to do the same in the future. But just in case my suspicions are correct: Mom, dad, please stay off the e-mail.

February 12, 1998

The Modern Protesters' Lament

And people say the younger generation doesn't care! Here is what anti-war demonstrators chanted last week at a college campus "international town hall" meeting on the topic of bombing Iraq: "One-two-three-four, we don't want your racist war!" Far out, man. Very groovy. If they yell it one more time I think I'm going to have an acid flashback. Where's my lava lamp?

Boy, were we ever wrong about the X Generation. These kids can cause quite a ruckus when they put their tattoos into it. With only six thousand in the audience at the college arena, the protesters numbered well over two dozen. Some say the dissidents were at least thirty-five strong. The Vietnam-era alumni from Berkeley must have been very impressed.

All I can say is, Bob Dylan was so right. The times, they have a changed. I keep waiting for a voiceover to tell us that "this 'Sixties Moment' was brought to you by Texaco, and other sponsors of the Gulf War." Then we can all chuckle at these lonely knuckleheads and get back to our margaritas. Can you imagine – those peaceniks are going to be managing our stock portfolios someday?

Today's kids obviously don't have the values and work ethic that their parents had. Because there was a time when this country knew how to throw a proper protest. Maybe we need to give today's youth a lesson on rebellion, because they just don't seem to get it. So listen up Xers, I'm only going over this once.

First of all, you guys need a leader. Abbie Hoffman is dead, so you're going to have to get your own. Here is a profile of the person you are looking for. Your leader should be a college dropout with an I.Q. over one-fifty who writes poetry, comes from a wealthy family, and bathes infrequently. Unfortunately, the Unabomber is already booked, and most of the other people who fit this description are currently negotiating good deals on the price of a truckload of anthrax.

Once you have a leader you need to unite. EVERYBODY must get stoned, remember? Having now twice invoked the legacy of Dylan, I must note that conspicuously absent at last week's "rally" was the cloud of bluish haze that must hover over any large gathering of students who intend to be taken seriously by The Man.

When you have a large enough group, you need to block the exits of any public forum where the topic is war, and sit on the floor. This will cause the listening audience to want to stampede over you immediately. Be careful not to get your nose rings tangled in their navel rings during the hysteria.

Now that you have inside position you have an element of power. Governmental persons of authority tend to feel very threatened by large masses of young people sitting on floors. Burly police officers will soon arrive and begin beating you with flashlights and nightsticks. Pandemonium will ensue and troops will be called in.

Some of your fellow protesters are likely to be shot dead while running from confused National Guard members who believe the security of the nation is in jeopardy because they don't like the music you listen to. The upside to this is that government-sponsored, tragically unnecessary deaths often inspire great songs from popular bands. So, don't lose your Walkman in the madness.

Once the funerals are over with and the wounded have come home from the hospitals you will want to memorialize your "movement" forever. You will want to frame Pulitzer Prize winning photographs of the carnage so that you can hang them someday in your law office. You'll want books written and movies produced that glamorize your plight. You will want all this so that you can assure yourself that you did something good, and that you changed the world in some positive way.

If a lot of people died in an international conflict despite your efforts, at least you will know you tried. And if you never again quite trust the country you live in, that would be understandable. But in thirty years or so, if you still think you can make a difference and you run for political office, and your opponent of tender years calls you a draft dodger because of your forgotten era anti-war stance, then you will know the true folly of your sentimental heart.

So just forget about Iraq and all those U.S. bombs, Generation X. Take your two dozen protesters and go rollerblading. You will look back in the years ahead and have none of the tragic memories and misspent energy to lament. But, hey, you'll still have those fine tattoos.

February 23, 1998

The Sprewell Amendment

Latrell Sprewell had his punishment for choking his coach dramatically reduced by an arbitrator last week. Days later a lottery employee in Connecticut went postal and killed four of his bosses in a deadly shooting spree (not to be confused with "Spree," which is Latrell's nickname). The Sprewell decision would make a lot more sense had the lottery killings occurred BEFORE the ruling. Then the arbitrator's logic could have been based on how mild-mannered Sprewell's actions really were.

Two different disgruntled employees, two different results. The question now is – when can an NBA player be fired by his team? If Sprewell had shot Coach P.J. Carlesimo, would that have been enough to warrant a pink slip?

The other question is – are sports a reflection of society, or is it vice versa? If the answer is the former choice, then Sprewell better have self-inflicted bruises on his neck because the lottery guy killed himself before being arrested. Now there's a guy who won't come crying about due process.

I don't know the answer to the first question. I suspect that shooting your coach in professional sports is probably at least enough to get you traded to the worst team in the league. In Sprewell's case he was already on a team contending for that title. You could only be sure that they really were the worst team – regardless of their win-loss record – after his teammates showed up en masse to support Sprewell at a televised conference.

The answer to the second question is much easier. Society imitates, emulates, and mimics sports. If you doubt that for one second, then go to any basketball court a couple of hours after Michael Jordan has played in a nationally televised game. See if you can spot just one guy out there who doesn't think he can beat a triple-team off the dribble by floating through the air from the foul line to the basket and switching hands just before finger-rolling the ball gently off the backboard. With his tongue sticking out.

On the playground, trying to be like Mike is only dangerous to the ego. The average weekend-warrior attempting such a feat has practiced it solely by watching Jordan perform it. Gravity comes quickly to those whose pre-game routine consists of washing down cheese puffs with root beer while prone on the sofa. According to recent emergency room studies, tongue lacerations are way up in the 1990's.

But what happens when we start trying to be like Spree? This could be cause for concern. Many of us do not have an arbitration clause in our contracts. Besides, an arbitrator's decision is not necessarily binding on other arbitrators.

Wouldn't it be nice if it were, though? If we all got to arbitrate our grievances, and the Sprewell decision was the law, people just might stop going postal – or lotto - on us. The more I think about it, the more I like this arbitrator guy.

If society has to imitate sports, the Sprewell decision is a great place to start. The new rule, then, is that choking your boss will cost you one year of work and pay. No subsidizing your existence by any governmental body. If you can get by without a paycheck for one fiscal turn of your job's calendar you can choke your boss for seven to ten seconds (the official count of the Sprewell incident) beginning now.

The new rule shall be known as the Sprewell Amendment. Bosses are hereby on notice. We are, after all, a civilized people in this country. Rare is the boss who truly deserves to be shot and killed. But rarer yet is the supervisory dictator of higher authority who does not deserve seven to ten seconds of good carotid throttling now and then. Personally, I would be squeezing somebody's windpipe right now if I weren't self-employed.

There are only two sub-rules to the new amendment.

(No rule is official without sub-rules that define and limit the original rule.) First, only you can choke your boss. Big brothers and hired thugs with extra-large hands are strictly prohibited.

There is one addendum to the first sub-rule. The boss you choke must be an actual boss, not an apparent boss. You may not strangle a co-worker who only thinks he's your boss.

Sub-rule number two prohibits constricting the breathing passage of an ex-boss. I know this takes a lot of the fun out of the Sprewell Amendment. But we can't have a complete free-for-all of neck wringing out there. So, you can only do the Lambada on the larynx of someone who presently signs, or is somehow responsible for you receiving, your paycheck.

I like the Sprewell Amendment. It could put an end to much of the mayhem caused by disgruntled workers. Phrases like, "He choked under pressure," will soon have a whole new meaning. Yes, some people are going to end up with long, unpaid vacations. But a lot of bosses are going to start paying a lot more attention at the Management-Employee Relations seminars.

March 9, 1998

Radar Love

When I was a kid, I spent many a day fishing with my grandfather. My grandfather was crippled with rheumatoid arthritis, but he rarely missed an outing on the boat. He was an amazing man in many respects, not the least of which was his unique method for putting bait on his hook. Because his fingers were weakened and bent at odd angles, he would sometimes put one end of a piece of fishbait in his teeth and tug it onto the hook with a clenched jaw. This was way before sushi restaurants became popular, so the technique never really caught on.

But the most amazing thing I remember about my grandfather was the day he said that he smelled rain. We were fishing about a mile offshore and the sun was shining. I chuckled and shook my head with all the wisdom of a twelve-year-old boy who recognizes the irrational statements of an old geezer idling the time away. Then I looked over my shoulder and saw the darkest, meanest squall line rolling towards us from the opposite direction that my grandfather was facing.

This is a lost art. The smelling of rain, that is. The "I feel it in my bones" predictions are gone also. Forget about the Farmer's Almanac. Now we have the "Weather Channel." Arthritic knees and sensitive sinuses are obsolete in the forecast world.

The Weather Channel has changed the world we live in. I used to hear the grizzled veterans who fished the piers and beaches talk about how the first nor'easter would bring the bluefish south. But the last time I was down by the docks a bunch of old-timers were sitting around waiting for the local forecast. On the eights, every hour. One of them lamented the lack of fishing action.

"What we need," he said, pointing at some circular squiggly lines on the screen, "is for this high-pressure system to push this ridge of warm air out into the gulf which would cause a thermal inversion and create turbulence along the coastline. Then we'll catch some fish."

"Ain't gonna happen," said a thin wrinkled gentleman who was sharpening a small knife with slow precision. He spit on the sharpening stone and pointed at Nebraska. "You see right there where the jet stream is getting pushed up north; that's caused by this stationary front which is sucking moisture out of the gulf and building a strong low-pressure presence that will tend to drift slowly north and east causing unusual amounts of snow in the Tennessee Valley."

It's not just the fishermen who are hooked on the Weather Channel. It's all of us. I used to love to watch a good storm out the biggest window in the house. But now I watch it on the television. I hunker down with the wife and kids and hit "favorite" on the remote control.

The color of bad weather used to be darkening shades of gray and purple in the sky. Now the darkness of the green on the radar screen excites us. Seeing a red or yellow blotch headed our way on the Doppler is almost as much fun as spotting an actual funnel cloud used to be. If this behavior were to carry over into other areas of our lives we could be in real trouble.

For example, if someone was getting murdered and all he wanted to do was watch the news to see what it looked like, this could be a problem. Or, what if we stopped cooking meals and just watched The Food Channel instead? "I'm hungry, mommy," would be followed by, "well, put on channel forty-eight then – but don't watch too long because the dinner show comes on in an hour."

Pretty soon people would stop going fishing. They would simply wait for some good nor'easter graphics to hit their region on the Weather Channel and then they would tune in to "The Outdoor World" and watch some excellent angling take place. If anybody nagged them about yardwork they could switch on "The Gardening Network" for an hour or two.

The only real worry we have anymore is that the cable

or the electricity might go out. And that is a possibility, because the radar is currently showing a band of heavy thunderstorms with frequent lightning strikes headed our way.

If my grandfather was still around today, he wouldn't be spending his time watching anything as silly as the Weather Channel. But he would know all about the coming storm. He would sit in the back of the boat like he always did. He would put his nostrils into the ocean breeze, spit out a morsel of bonito belly, and say, "It smells like El Nino."

Tallahassee Democrat – March 12, 1998

Killing Time

Man, I'm busy. How about you? Yeah, that's what I thought. Busy, busy, busy. Well, it was good talking to you. Let's get together sometime and talk about the stuff we used to do when we weren't so busy. Those were the days, huh?

How did we get so busy, anyway? Never mind. I really don't have time to hear it. I have about ten phone calls I need to make right now to people who have not returned my previous phone calls. They are all going to tell me how busy they are. It would sure save me a lot of time if they wouldn't bother.

One of the things I've noticed now that I'm so busy is that I don't have as many friends as I used to. My friends are even busier than I am, so I've lost touch with many of them. I find myself spending a lot of my free time making new friends. New friends are usually not as busy as old friends. But it takes a lot of time to make a new friend, so I'm busier than ever.

I spend a lot of the time when I'm with new friends telling them about my old friends. There are some great stories to tell. Those guys were the best. Sometimes my new friends like my stories so much that they call my old friends and then they become friends. When that happens, my new friends often become too busy to maintain the friendship with me.

I almost called one of my old friends a few days ago. I had the phone in my hand, my beer on the end table, and my butt in an armchair. I was very relaxed. It should have been a great time to call an old friend and get caught up.

Then I started thinking about all the things I needed to do. Just because I wasn't doing anything didn't mean I wasn't busy. And a call to an old friend is a thirty or forty-minute gig, minimum. So, I spent twenty-five minutes thinking about all the stuff I needed to do. Then I spent ten minutes looking out the window wondering where I would find the time to get these things done. I made a mental note to call my old friend when I wasn't so busy.

Another friend e-mails me regularly that we should have lunch together soon. That's an awfully nice thing to do. When you are as busy as the two of us are, an e-mail suggesting lunch together is just as good as actually having lunch together used to be.

Lunch is just such a busy time of day. I personally eat lunch every day. My friend with the e-mail doesn't look like he has missed many lunches either. But to have lunch together takes so much time. Two people just cannot eat lunch as fast as one person. Besides, I get most of my work done during lunch. The rest of the day I'm answering e-mails and thinking about making phone calls.

Something has got to go, because I'm too darn busy. There aren't that many friends left, so that can't be the problem. I have a gym membership, but I haven't been there in months. I do think about going a lot, though. All the stress from worrying about not going to the gym can't be good for you. I'll have to put that at the top of my list of things not to do anymore.

And then there's this article. Yes, this one I'm writing now. I'm really way too busy to be writing this. And you are way too busy to be reading it. What the hell is the matter with us?

In the time it took to write this I could have typed up an entire list of things I need to do. Then I could have typed a list of things I'm too busy to do anymore. The problem is the second list would look an awful lot like the first list.

But I would probably be too busy to ever read them anyway.

March 23, 1998

Guns R Us

Children are not supposed to come home from school in body bags. Teachers are not supposed to earn their meager pay by stepping in front of bullets meant for sixth graders. Thirteen-year-old boys are not supposed to methodically set up mass-murdering firing squads when their girlfriends dump them.

March 24, 1998, was not supposed to happen to Jonesboro, Arkansas.

Or was it? Is it possible that the events in Jonesboro were just a logical extension of the illogical world we live in? Mindless violence has become so passé that we are becoming ever more hard-pressed to feign shock over a recap of the day's bloodbath. Prepubescent snipers are enough to raise our eyebrows, but we all know that a six-year-old with an Uzi is out there somewhere just waiting to make a statement worthy of CNN's top story of the day.

This is the world we have created. We love violence and

we can't get enough. Ever since Alfred Nobel invented dynamite humans have been enthralled with blowing each other up and blowing each other away. Americans, particularly, are fascinated by explosive pastimes. We lead the league in dropping bombs. And we have plenty more where those came from, pointing at anybody who looks suspicious. The whole world knows that if they mess with us, we'll blow them right off the planet.

Guns? Guns are kid's stuff. Adults are out there filling moving vans full of gunpowder and leaving knapsack time bombs full of nails near Olympic events. Explosives capable of mass destruction have become the mature person's weapons of choice. Guns are only acceptably efficient enough for people too small to get on Space Mountain.

Somebody interviewed in Jonesboro blamed the entertainment industry for inspiring the mayhem. Television, movies, and computer games. Rap music; now there's a real killer. Anybody who believes this theory should be riddled with Hollywood bullets by a bad guy character from the last Seagal-Willis-Van Damme-Stallone movie that grossed over one hundred million box-office dollars.

The entertainment industry sells what we want to buy. Americans crave violence. We order it in bulk, and we prefer it wholesale. We are not a "Full Monty" kind of crowd. We are a "Die Hard or I'll Kill You Some More" audience. We never get enough carnage in the real world.

Bloodletting movies and songs and video games are just to help us fill the void.

Nobody is going to take America's guns away. We are a nation of second amendment experts who have dissected this sacrosanct provision with a kamikaze interpretation that defies civilized logic. And nobody better say that we are stupid just because we have no idea what freedom the third amendment speaks to. Call us names and we might have to plug you with a steel-jacketed, hollow point, crosshatched, armor-piercing, terminator bullet. That's right, we bad.

Exactly how skewed how has our reasoning on weapons become? When I heard about the Jonesboro shootings I remembered a column written by Tallahassee Democrat editorial page editor, Andrea Brunais. The column appeared in the Democrat back on November 16, 1997. Brunais wrote about the ill effects of handgun control, citing a Florida State University professor who had studied the subject for over twenty years.

According to the Brunais spin, handgun control proponents have been hiding the "dirty little secret" for years that anti-gun laws are ineffective. In fact, Brunais had cold, hard facts – although not as cold or as hard as the Jonesboro news – to support her newly embraced theory.

Brunais' statistical data showed that two-and-a-half million people a year use handguns for defensive purposes, while only one million crimes occur each year in which an offender carries a gun. If we do a Venn diagram with these numbers the results are rather peculiar. It seems there are one-and-a-half million people out there using a gun to defend themselves against unarmed offenders.

This may not be a good thing. Brunais does not explain exactly what the defensive purpose of pulling a gun on an unarmed offender is, nor does she mention that using a weapon in this situation may be illegal. This of course, would make the defender a criminal and would help even up the stats, but I'm confused enough over these numbers.

Brunais left the barn door on logic open even wider when she quoted something called the "Almanac of American Politics." The almanac explained that since muggers target those who don't have guns, allowing law-abiding citizens to carry concealed weapons results in lower crime rates.

Let's apply that reasoning to Jonesboro, or to the school that your children attend. Bullies, punks, and snipers are much more likely to target students that don't carry weapons. So, if we just let the "good" kids pack pistols in their lunchboxes we won't have any more unexplainable bloodshed on campuses.

When otherwise rational people begin drawing the dubious conclusions set forth in the Brunais column, it is easy to see where the solution lies for all of us. Get a gun. In fact, get the family pack.

Remember, though, that criminals will not know you have a concealed weapon unless you use it. So, shoot anybody that offends you. This will not only lower crime rates, it will also teach your children a valuable lesson.

Tallahassee Democrat – April 9, 1998

Smoking in the Boys' Room

The kids are all right. Really, I mean it. I have to admit that I have been worried about the young generation. I read about gangs, and guns on campus, and low-test scores, and teenage pregnancies, and I say to myself – "these kids today!"

But salvation has come for the children from the unlikeliest of places. Cigarette makers have ponied up fifty million dollars and handed it to Florida teenagers to spend on creating anti-smoking advertisements.

Whew! I feel a lot better, how about you? Once the kids get the message out to other kids that smoking is no good for you, I expect the rest of the problems will take care of themselves.

Of course, it's not going to be easy to get teenagers to stop smoking. That's why they need fifty million. Kids have been smoking tobacco – and other leafy products – since Tom Sawyer's day, and maybe even before that.

There's a lot of legacy involved.

But the teens are not pulling any punches. I saw one of their early efforts in yesterday's newspaper. The full-page ad was in the front-page section where it was sure to be seen by dozens of high schoolers. The ad pictured a student in a classroom wearing a ski mask and holding a list of demands of cigarette makers that appears to be slightly longer than a senior term paper.

The idea presented in the ad was that kids have been hostages of the tobacco companies for too long, and now it's the kids' turns to make the demands. Personally, I thought the metaphor got a little tangled in the allegory, but we're not grading papers here. The theme of the campaign is "truth," which has nice wholesome ring to it.

Truth. If you say it out loud it does have a good solid feel. It's a high-quality one-syllable word. So, let's talk about the truth.

The truth is, fifty million dollars' worth of anti-smoking advertisements created by the very people that the ads target is not going to stop teenage smoking. You know it, I know it, and the boys in the bathroom know it. The money would be better spent on new toilet seats and improved ventilation in the quintessential smoking lounges on campus.

Put the new teen-created anti-smoking crusade down at the bottom of the interminable lists of ideas that have failed previously. Detentions, suspensions, conferences, restrictions, confinement, corporal punishment, hard labor. Not a success story in the bunch.

Teenage smoking is the social equivalent of the Vietnam War. It's a fight we can't win. The kids not only have home field advantage, they have the absence of sound logic to fall back on at all times. When hard-pressed, they can't give one good reason why they smoke cigarettes. Argue with that for a while.

We don't need to advocate teen smoking, but it might not be such a bad idea to accept it. There really are better things to spend the money on. I'm certain of it.

Why don't we start with those low test scores I mentioned earlier? It is possible that kids could do better if our classrooms were less crowded. If we spent more money on textbooks, supplies, and classroom technology we might see positive results. Higher salaries for educators might create a larger pool of applicants from which to select the people we entrust with teaching our children.

I'm all for taking the money from the cigarette makers. While we're at it why don't we ask producers of other unhealthy products to ante up. The cola bottlers responsible for bad teeth and high sugar levels should be invited to the table. And fast food burger corporations who are clogging up adolescent arteries should be dealt in also.

But let's spend the money where we know it will do some good. Children are innately hungry for knowledge. Fifty million dollars is a lot of lunch money.

April 14, 1998

The Armchair Quarterback

Like millions of Americans, I tuned in to ESPN on April 14 to watch the forum discussion on race relations in sports. Like millions of Americans, I think it's very important to listen to the President of the United States and other prominent persons offer insights on the delicate and troublesome topic of race. Like many of those million Americans I also find it much easier to pay attention when I know that sports updates will scroll across the bottom of the screen every fifteen minutes.

Here are some other observations from the socially conscious armchair.

***

The best segment of the evening took place before the panel was introduced. ESPN did a lead-in showing footage of Charles Barkley speaking to a group of elementary school children on the topic of racism. No explanation was offered of why Barkley was chosen to impart his always-suspect wisdom before an audience of tender impression. Barkley has previously made emphatically clear his position that athletes are not role models. He has punctuated those remarks by throwing a man in a restaurant through a plate glass window, and by spitting on a courtside fan.

But on this day, it was Sir Charles who took the lumps. When Barkley tried to impose his skewed version of human traits on the room full of little people he caught an elbow of intelligence from a kid in the third row.

The child responded with an unflinching "yes," when Barkley asked the class if his statement that blacks could jump higher than whites was racist. The student, who was also African-American, explained to Barkley that his conclusion was wrong because he had not conducted the kind of scientific survey necessary to support it.

Barkley, pursuing the truth more relentlessly than a rebound headed for a cement-footed Caucasian, went on to defend his hypothesis by stating in equally unscientific fashion that blacks were better basketball players than whites. The supporting survey, he implied, was conducted during the last twenty-five years of jumping over and scoring around white players who just didn't measure up.

If the child had been older and more experienced, he might have asked Barkley if those weren't the same kind of stereotypical statements that have previously caused so much trouble for Al Campanis, Jimmy the Greek, Fuzzy Zoeller, and Reggie White. Instead, in the perfect innocence of early adolescence, the child simply explained that almost any white kid at his school could jump higher and play basketball better than he could.

Undaunted in his inimitable ignorance, Barkley gave no indication that he understood that he had just been schooled rather badly in a one-on-one contest of wits with a grade-schooler.

***

At some point during the panel discussion it occurred to me that I could not recall ever seeing a U.S. President in a live forum that was interrupted by commercials. How much money could be raised if the White House adopted this policy for presidential addresses and news conferences?

Maybe we could finance the next war if we pause during the State of the Union for a word from Miller Lite.

***

It would be interesting to hear an explanation of why, on such a large panel of speakers, only one woman was chosen to participate. Title IX has had a profoundly positive effect on collegiate athletics and academics. But it is still apparent that without legal motivation the boys are mighty reluctant to let the girls play.

In the end, it is that same theme that keeps race an issue long after the enlightenment that civil rights acts should have brought. When the men won't include the women, the same social sabotage is at work that keeps minorities from inclusion.

Status quo seven, human rights zero.

* * *

All in all it was a very pretty evening. Blacks and whites discussing an issue as if the problems had been identified and steps were in place to correct them. It was like a team of surgeons inspecting a giant scab on a patient. A few of them stroked their chins thoughtfully, and a couple of them picked at the edges gently.

But nobody kicked the bloody crust off and exposed the true extent of the wound.

I got the impression, from deep in the folds of my conscientious armchair, that we all know the truth. The truth is not very pretty at all. I would get up and talk about the truth myself. But, man, that chair is comfortable.

April 23, 1998

Every Chapter Tells a Story, Don't It?

I can't make it to the school tomorrow, and that's too bad. I was invited, along with several other big people, to speak to a group of children, kindergarten through fourth grade, about reading. I was supposed to tell the kids a story about how reading affected my life, and then read a passage to them from a book of my choosing. I can't make it because of a scheduling conflict. But I would sure like to tell my story.

My story would have to start in first grade. The only two things I remember about first grade are the afternoon naps and learning how to read. "See Jip. See Jip run. Run, Jip, run." Now that was good stuff. Nothing too complicated, just good, clean prose. Read a couple of pages like that and the next thing you know you're out in the yard rolling in the grass with a small dog.

Oh, and I remember a girl I met in our reading group. There were four or five of us in the "Blue" group, but I still remember the blonde girl that sat across from me and read with such enthusiasm. I remember her eyes and how they always seemed to be smiling. We had a good time reading in the Blue group.

Once I learned how to read, I couldn't get enough. Over the next two years I ripped through a bookcase full of Dr. Seuss. I still talk like a Seussian character from time to time, but only when I'm completely thrgglmphed.

When I found Aesop's Fables, I read them over and over again. At the end of each fable was a little note called "The moral of the story." Just in case you didn't get the significance of the fox who couldn't reach the sour grapes. Sometimes I think all stories should have a little note at the end called "The moral of the story."

My favorite story about how reading affected my life happened in fourth grade. Black children were not allowed to attend my elementary school until they reached the fourth grade. Nobody ever gave a reason for this that I remember. It was just a fact of life in my part of the world in 1967.

On the first day of class in fourth grade the teacher handed everyone a book and spent her day doing some kind of paperwork. The teacher had a reputation for being mean, and she looked like she was mad at something all the time. I remember getting finished with my book fairly quickly and sitting there with nothing to do. I was afraid to raise my hand and ask for another book so I just sat there quietly.

After a while I noticed that the kid in the desk across from me had finished early also. But he was black, and I had never spoken to a black kid before. I didn't know this teacher, I didn't know this kid, and I didn't know this color. So, I sat quietly with nothing to do.

And then the black kid held out his book and asked me if I wanted to swap. I handed him my book and he handed me his book. He told me his name and I told him my name. Neither one of us got in any trouble.

We read a lot in that class, and me and that black kid traded a lot of books. He never made it over to my house to play, and I never ventured over to his neighborhood, but I always thought of us as friends. We both read the same books so there was always something in common.

It sure would be fun to tell that story at the school tomorrow. Maybe I'll try again to rearrange my schedule. But if I can't make it I'll tell that story to my two boys when they get a little older. I'll probably tell it to them over and over again, like a good fable.

I'll tell my kids the story about first grade and learning how to read, too. I'll tell them about the Blue group and how much fun we used to have. With any luck, my boys will have the same enthusiasm for reading that the blonde girl that sat across from me used to have.
They already have her smiling eyes.

Moral of the story: There is nothing in the world like a good book with a happy ending.

April 27, 1998

Songs from the Bad Chair

Somewhere out there I have two brothers. I don't hear from them too often. We used to hang out occasionally when I lived a lot closer to them, but not enough to make anybody believe we actually cared for each other. Which we probably do. I think.

There may be a very good reason why my relationship with my brothers is so indifferent. If there is, I've never been able to figure it out. But I have always been curious about it. I often wondered if, since I'm the oldest of the three, it could be my fault somehow. Maybe I handed out one noogie too many way back when.

For a long time, I thought I would never really understand why my two brothers and I are not close. At family gatherings I would put my arms around them and say, "You guys are like the brothers I never had."

Then my wife and I had two children, fifteen months apart. Two boys. Ha, I thought, brothers! I decided immediately that I would conduct a study. I would observe their behavior and watch for signs that indicated any kind of emotional dissonance. By the time my boys reached their mid-thirties I figured I would understand the dynamics of my relationship with my own two brothers.

Seven months later, the study is over. I would like to take a brief moment here to apologize to my brothers. It is actually quite remarkable that they ever let me get anywhere near them once they acquired motor skills. I understand now that no real love exists between any brothers in the world. If two or more brothers appear to be close it is only a devious facade perpetrated by the younger brothers until vengeance can be had.

Seven months ago, our second son was born. At the hospital, our first son was so happy to meet his new brother that he ripped the beanie cap off the little one's head and tugged it onto his own. "Mine!" he shouted. And so, my study began.

This was not a controlled, scientific study. I decided very early that I would do everything in my power to ensure that these two boys would love each other and become friends for life.

My older boy destroyed that notion on the three-month anniversary of his brother's birth by pulling him off his bath seat and submerging the little man's head in six inches of water that ended abruptly at a very unforgiving bathtub floor. Big brother, being older and wiser by fifteen months, likes to sagely point out in the ensuing hysteria that often follows such an event that, "The baby cryin'."

Yes, the baby is crying, I say. The baby is crying because you were standing on his head. The baby is crying because you elbowed him in the face. Because you kicked him, shoved him, slapped him, and bit him.

I assume this behavior is a genetic trait that is found in all members of the sadistic species known in the scientific community as "boys." I pause again to say to each of my brothers, "Sorry, man."

My wife and I have tried to prevent this systematic abuse. The rules have been clearly written in the coloring book. A ten-inch, stuffed Pooh Bear has had many a talk with the big brother.

We even have a chair we send him to for punishment. The "Bad Chair." I'm not sure you can foster a lot of brotherly love by sending the offending child to the Bad Chair, but it seems to buy a little time. The Bad Chair is completely effective in stopping the targeted behavior for exactly the amount of time that the child stays in the Bad Chair.

The funny thing is, I don't have any memory of inflicting random and casual pain upon my brothers. But the study doesn't lie. Big brothers punish little brothers. It's a fact of life.

And little brothers remember. That's why they seldom call, never respond to e-mail, and always have something better to do than invite you over for dinner when you're in town. These are just self-defense mechanisms that develop in little brothers long before the soft spot on their head closes up.

And big brothers? What can I say? We are what we are. For example, my older son just yanked a toy out of my younger son's hands and hit him on the head with it. That's five minutes in the Bad Chair. If I squeeze way over, there's room for him right next to me.

Gadsden County Times May, 1998
Tallahassee Democrat – May 10, 1999
Big Apple Parent Magazine – May 1999

Yard For Sale

If you want a true evaluation of your net worth, have a yard sale. I guarantee, you are not worth as much as you thought. This is because the things you own are not worth what you paid for them. Having a yard sale is the quickest way to understand today's economy, which is to say it is the fastest way to figure out why you are always in debt.

I found out last Saturday. I spent three hours under a very large oak tree watching my possessions devalue faster than the peso in the early nineties. It was an important lesson. A quick comparison of my credit card balances with the net return from the reselling of the items that caused the credit card balances showed that my buying skills never properly developed.

I hope I remember this lesson next time I go shopping. Throwing a yard sale right before a trip to the mall is equivalent to visiting a slaughterhouse while eating a knockwurst. It should cause at a least a slight diminishment of appetite.

Yard sales are a vital component of this country's economy. There was a time when people bought goods based only on need, and then they used the goods until the items were completely worn out. This behavior lead to the Great Depression. People lived in poverty while listening to radios with no dials and wearing shoes with holes in them.

Then came the New Deal. The New Deal was a political manifesto designed to stimulate the economy by encouraging people to craft cardboard signs advertising yard sales where they would sell items they had recently purchased. Yard sales were an immediate hit. People began rummaging through their houses looking for items they had not used for several hours. If the batteries in the radio died, a yard sale was born.

There are several rules that apply to selling your belongings at a yard sale. It is much less painful to participate if you know these rules going in.

The first rule is that any particular item should be priced by the seller at half the value that the seller actually thinks the item is worth. So, a lamp that cost $150.00 that the seller thinks he can get $30.00 for should be priced at $15.00. This allows the shrewd buyer to offer $2.00 and settle at $3.50.

Using this formula, anyone can easily see how yard

sales help stimulate the nation's economy. The seller now has three bucks – the buyer didn't have quarters so the price was rounded down – to replace a $150.00 lamp that is still accumulating interest on a platinum credit card.

The second rule of yard sales is that your stuff is worth its highest value before you bring it out of the house. Buyers always pass up the displayed, priced items, and head for things you are still unpacking. For example, a pair of boots that is missing one boot can be sold for seven dollars if the solo boot has not yet been placed among the sale items.

The third rule is simply an extension of the second rule. Any item depreciates in value exponentially every time a potential buyer looks at it but doesn't buy it. If more than three people look at an item without buying it, the item is worthless and should be removed from the yard sale before it diminishes the value of other items.

The fourth rule of yard sales is probably the most intriguing. Buyers would rather pay $2.00 for broken, cracked, faded, worthless items than pay $5.00 for a state of the art toaster that has never been out of the box. In fact, never-used items only draw suspicious glances from buyers. The seller should always take the toaster out of the box and hit it several times with a rusty hammer to enhance its value.

The fifth rule of yard sales is the most important to learn. You are not going to make enough money selling your unwanted belongings to pay off all your bills and start a new life on the West Coast. You might make enough for a take-out pizza and a six-pack, but you'll probably need to bring quarters with you to make it.

When the yard sale is over and you're schlepping the unwanted items that couldn't be priced low enough back into the house, and you're tired and sweaty and depressed, remember this. Your net worth before a yard sale is exactly equal to Donald Trump's net worth during a yard sale.

May 11, 1998

The Golden Rulers

A dream came true for the Florida legislature this year. They woke up one day and found $184 million dollars in their wallets. It was a glorious day. Legislators sang and danced and ran up to each other saying, "Hey, is that $184 million dollars in your pocket, or are you just happy to see me?"

To celebrate their good fortune the lawmakers ate ambrosia and drank mead late into the night. Then they remembered that they had work to do.

"No problem!" came the cry from the chorus of senators.

"Let us take this money and make wonderful laws!" shouted the gaggle of representatives. And they all held hands and pranced to the lawmaking hall. This was a very good dream.

It was in this mood of merriment and jubilation that the 1998 Florida legislative session convened. $184 million dollars was stacked neatly in the middle of the room for all to see. Everyone wanted to spend the money as wisely and efficiently as possible. But it quickly became apparent that this would not be easy.

"I make a motion," said a well-respected senator with a big belly, "that we use the money to make sure that that the electric chair remains the official means of executing prisoners in our great state."

"Yes, yes!" cried the Gaggle.

"We concur," called the Chorus.

But the pile of money remained. The Gaggle murmured and the Chorus shuffled uneasily. A representative from Two Egg stood up to explain.

She pointed to a sheet of statistical data and said, "Yes, it will cost Florida many more millions of dollars to continue executing prisoners than to abolish the death penalty. But those are long-term effects and this money must be spent by midnight or we shall lose it all."

There was a roomful of oohs and ahs. Then a senator from Eustis stood. "Let us rename the Florida Turnpike," he boomed. "I hereby move that we rename the turnpike 'Ronald Reagan Memory Lane.'"

This created a stir among the politocrats and shouting ensued.

"Have you forgotten that Reagan was once a Democrat who supported abortion rights?" yelled a Republican from Micanopy.

"Have you forgotten that legislators once promised that the turnpike would be a toll-free road within twenty years of its conception?" mused a closet Libertarian from Umatilla.

The senator from Eustis waved his hands. "President Reagan does not remember being a Democrat any more than we remember that the turnpike was paid off a long time ago."

Confusion followed and the bill was quickly made into law. But the pile of money remained. The bean counter from Two Egg stood again. "Last year," she said, "we passed a law mandating that any changing of the name of the Florida Turnpike must paid for by raising the tolls."

"Ooh!" cried the Chorus. "We forgot."

"Ahh," whispered the Gaggle. "We didn't remember."

"Then what can we spend the money on?" asked the senator with the big belly. He pointed his belly at the bean counter from Two Egg.

"Let's give it to Big Business," shouted someone from the back of the Gaggle.

The bean counter shook her head. "We already gave them $100 million dollars, plus protection from consumer lawsuits."

The Chorus huddled. The Gaggle discussed. The clock crept towards midnight and the music from "Final Jeopardy" played in the background. Then the senator with the big belly made a motion.

"Let's keep it," he said, waving his hand in dismissal at the pile of money. "Let us reward ourselves with this booty for all the hard work and public service we have provided."

Eyebrows raised and a silent hush filled the hall. The bean counter looked thoughtful. She scribbled on a pad for a moment and then she smiled. "I think it can be done," she said. "But to keep it we have to give it back."

This created chaos. Screaming and kicking began, and one representative held his breath and turned blue. It had become almost as ugly as an election speech in November when the bean counter whispered a word into the ear of the big belly senator.

The senator smiled, patted his belly and whispered in the ear of the lawmaker next to him. Word spread like wildfire and soon everyone was merry again. Then a representative from Hialeah came back from the bathroom and panicked.

"The money is gone!" he yelled. And indeed, it was. "Where did it go," he cried.

The Chorus and the Gaggle held hands and sang in unison, "Re-election!"

Tallahassee Democrat – May 14, 1998

Nuclear Reaction

It's too late for me to buy a gun. All my right-wing friends have had their conservative little fingers on the trigger for too long. I will never be able to match their savvy of these hand-held weapons. Nor will I be able to catch up to their stockpile. They have more guns, and they have bigger guns. Everybody does. That's why I'm building a nuclear warhead.

I will be conducting a test of my nuclear capabilities in my backyard next Friday, so you may want to stay out of my neighborhood for a while. Not that there will be any danger to anyone. I will be exploding my first nuke inside a bomb shelter built in the early 1960's, so it should be very safe.

Safety is what my bomb is all about. I have been wallowing in my pinko, liberal philosophies too long. All my Republican friends say so. The only reason they have tolerated my left-wing, anti-war, flower-in-the-gun-barrel politics for this long is because I cook a mean plate of clam linguine. Now, I'm going to make them proud.

I do expect a little fallout, so to speak. The CIA, and other oppressive government agencies, probably will not be happy with my activities. And somewhere out there in America, the other guy who doesn't currently own a weapon will be despondent. He will probably send me an e-mail with a quote from a Joni Mitchell song in it. Yes, we'll be getting back to the garden – right after this mushroom cloud drifts away.

I do not expect any meaningful resistance, however. I have the second amendment on my side, for one thing. I admit, I never really understood this little beauty in my free-loving, give-peace-a-chance days. But now that I'm thinking safety first, old Number Two is my new best friend.

Besides the National Rifle Association, that is. Where have these guys been all my life? They always have the best slogans! I've been working on a couple of new ones while I build my warhead. My first one is: "If nuclear bombs are outlawed, only India will have nuclear bombs." Damn, I'm funny sometimes.

But here's my favorite: "Nuclear Bombs Don't Kill People." Can't argue with that, can you? I have to admit, I stole the idea during dinner the other night off a clam-scarfing Federalist who was railing on about the latest high school shooting frenzy. "I can't wait to hear the leftist crybabies explaining how inanimate objects took all those lives," he said, spitting out a littleneck in his passion.

I handed back his clam and nodded sagely. Then I experienced a sort of pasta-induced Epiphany. I stared too long at a candle on the table and drifted into a non-somnambulist vision. I saw myself flying through a tunnel where the walls were graffitied with hippie slogans and posters of Woodstock. At the end of the tunnel stood Barry Goldwater holding the candle. As I got closer the candle turned into a nuclear warhead.

The cork popped on a bottle of Chianti and I snapped out of it. My right-wing dinner guest was discussing the comfort of being well armed. He had come home once, in his pro-gun control days, and found a burglar inside. Unarmed as he was in those unenlightened days, he could only wrestle the burglar to the ground and phone the police. Now he owns five handguns, which are stashed around the house, and in his car. "Burglar Begones, I call them," he said, tapping a finger confidently against his temple.

"Hmmm," I muttered skeptically, still torn between the obvious message of my vision and the ballot I once cast for Paul Tsongas in a presidential primary. "But what happens," I asked, "if you come home and find Pakistan in your living room?"

I didn't hear his answer. I knew then what I had to do. To be safe. To be very, very, safe.

Many American households already have stockpiles of firearms larger than most third-world countries. Smaller and smaller starving nations are skipping the gunpowder and going straight for the plutonium. Sometime soon there will be a meeting in the middle. I decided I would get there first.

When I explained my plan to my Republican friend, he refused to finish his dessert. "You're insane!" he cried as he slipped his shoulder holster on. "You, sir," he stated while checking his spare clip, "are a menace to us all." He grabbed a doggie bag of angel hair and cherrystones in a white sauce and stomped out the door.

I stared at the candle and whispered after him, "Be safe, my little dove. Be very, very safe."

May 25, 1998

McHugh

I'm no Woodward and Bernstein. I would rather make things up than investigate them. But I do like a good conspiracy theory. I often suspect that there is something going on that they are not telling us about. You know what I mean. UFO's, moon landings, grassy knolls. And then there's McHugh.

In case you missed it, Florida State University law school professor William McHugh was suspended from his teaching duties on June 11, 1998. He was accused of exposing himself to a female student in his office. According to the account I read, McHugh was attempting to show off a scar from a hernia operation when he inadvertently revealed a bit more. So, they suspended him.

Those of us who had McHugh for a professor usually just called him McHugh. His persona defied nicknames. If someone asked whom you had for contracts, all you had to say was "McHugh." Many students would use the same voice inflection that Seinfeld used to refer to Newman.

So, he wasn't the most popular professor on campus. He was a colorful guy, though, and he liked to pepper his lectures with indelicate remarks and anecdotes. He liked to use profanity as much as he liked to incorporate arcane Latin terminology into his discussion. Some students took offense at his abrasive style and opted out of his class. Others enjoyed his racy raconteuring and took every course he taught. Most that were assigned his contracts class – a mandatory first year course – weathered the storm with ambivalence.

I like McHugh. In the classroom he can be mean, nasty, hostile, and, by some standards, disgusting. He can also be funny, entertaining, and interesting. But he was never boring, which would be a kind and gentle way to describe the teaching styles of several of his faculty peers. I found I learned a lot more in the courses that I was awake for. McHugh also has a big heart. He takes care of those who suffered his presence. He wrote me a letter of recommendation once that was embarrassingly laudatory in its description of my attributes. I got the job. He has done the same for many others.

I could call him tomorrow with a question, and he would take the time to answer. He would probably also take the time to cuss liberally, and he might make remarks that many would consider politically incorrect. McHugh could guest-host for Bill Maher anytime.

Of course, these last traits are the exact ones that have gotten McHugh into trouble many times in the past. Many, many times. But they were never enough to hang him. It's just not that easy to fire a tenured professor. It takes a little help.

Enter the indecent exposure charge. But I suspect that even that accusation was not enough to put a noose on the old man. Based on the description of events supplied by the accusing student, it would not necessarily follow – even if the accusations were proved true – that a tenured professor with twenty-five years at an institution would be removed from his position over such an indiscretion. To make such a drastic move you really need to have public opinion on your side.

Gather round, fellow conspiracists. See if you smell something peculiar here. (No scatological references please, not even in eulogy.)

Remember our plot. Crusty, aging, somewhat less than benign professor, who has embarrassed the administration so many times that the mere mention of his name sends a chill down their softened spines. He had outlived his usefulness years ago, but nobody ever had the temerity to put the noose over his head.

Judging by the way McHugh was finally ousted, it doesn't look like anybody in charge has developed any courage yet.

On Tuesday, June 9, the St. Petersburg Times ran a front-page story detailing some of McHugh's past troubles. This was a bit curious. Front page coverage about a two-year-old scandal concerning allegations of sexist and racist remarks that had died quietly. No mention of the new allegation.

Even more curious was the fact that the story was not picked up by the hometown newspaper, Tallahassee Democrat.

Not that the Democrat was necessarily being scooped by a cross-state rival. It was just that the Democrat chose that particular Tuesday to run an article highlighting the efforts of FSU's law program in recruiting minority and disadvantaged students. A person reading this article just might think the law school was a real credit to the community. We wouldn't want anyone to ruin that image, would we?

The headline that ran above that article is worth noting in retrospect. Bizarre coincidence, or humorous foreshadowing? You decide. It said: "FSU Exposes Students to Practice of Law."

Moving forward. The Democrat runs the story on Wednesday, June 10, that the St Pete Times ran on Tuesday. Front page, top headline. Again, old news is the big story of the day. There was still no mention of the new accusation. (Meanwhile, buried on page three of the local section in the same Wednesday paper is a story about an adjunct instructor at FSU who had been arrested the day before on a charge of extortion. The instructor allegedly forced a student to perform a sexual act or risk being failed in the course. Am I just paranoid, or is there something wrong with the location of these articles?)

In legalspeak, the foundation had now been laid to introduce the new evidence. Build the character of the institution on Tuesday. Uncover a flaw in the character on Wednesday. Spring the surprise witness on Thursday. And so it went. Front-page headlines on Thursday, June 11, documented these scandalous new charges that amazingly surfaced just one day after crack reporting had rehashed some old ugliness. Friday's headline announced McHugh's suspension.

It was a team effort, but the barnacle was scraped from the hull. Clear sailing ahead. Like I said, McHugh wasn't always pretty to be around. But he was never as ugly as this hatchet job.

It just goes to show how quickly things can happen when high-ranking officials get a little cooperation from the press. Conspiracy? Well, it's just a theory, but it works for me.

June 21, 1998

Water Colored World

I don't want to be mislabeled, so I should let you know that I'm a white male. Labels are very in right now. Especially ones that identify color. At other times of political or social unrest you might want to know if I am gay or straight, liberal or conservative, pro-choice or pro-life. But right now, my most important characteristic is my color.

I'm not likely to get an argument on that from anyone in Quincy these days. In this small city west of Tallahassee, many residents are black, while many others are white. I know these details because I read the Tallahassee Democrat, which has been reporting on some political infighting taking place recently in Quincy.

What happened, according to the Democrat, was that some black commissioners in Quincy fired some white people with good jobs and gave most of the good jobs to black people, although some of the good jobs went to other white people. The Tallahassee Democrat supplies the names of these people also, but it's pretty clear that the importance of the story lies in the labels attached to the names. To know the players, you have to know their color.

Some black people in Quincy are not happy with the actions of the black commissioners, but other blacks are pleased with the results. The white people seem to be united in their unhappiness with the black commissioners. I would say that this could get ugly, but when newspapers from neighboring cities are reporting on your problems, it's already a bit unattractive, yes?

President Clinton's national dialogue on race continues. I'm glad we decided to talk this out, aren't you?

Meanwhile, in Jasper, Texas, three white men allegedly chained a black man to their truck and dragged him behind it until the black man was dead, and then some. The white men – also apparently afraid to be mislabeled – sported various tattoos identifying themselves as white supremacists.

The residents of Jasper are troubled. They don't want to be labeled. An Associated Press story quoted several of the citizens who commented on the atrocity. Herman Wright, who is black; David Barnett, who is white; and Alene Dunn, who is white, all felt compelled to defend their community. If the AP hadn't identified their color, I would have guessed that Alene was a black woman. I can't think of any difference it would have made had I spent the rest of my life with that mistaken belief.

Sheriff Billy Rowles – who is white – called Jasper "typical middle America." That statement seems about right to me. Typical middle America is a place where blacks and whites reside and work in the same area. Asians and Hispanics, too. And once in a while, for no apparent reason other than the color of skin, somebody dies a horrible death.

Quincy doesn't claim to be typical Middle America. Quincy has been striving for a much more glorious label. "All America City" is the goal. If you go to the city of Quincy website you can learn all about it.

At the top of the webpage it still says Ken Cowen is city manager. But Cowen – who is white – was suspended from his job by three black commissioners. They will probably fire him soon. At least they didn't chain him to a car and drag him down the road. Of course, that wouldn't be appropriate in an All-America City. It's much more suitable for typical middle America.

I'm kind of confused, because I live in Tallahassee. As far as I know, Tallahassee has not labeled itself as either typical or All America. But it was reported recently that two white kids at a local high school published a newsletter that aimed racial epithets and death threats at a black teacher. So, I'm going to go ahead and label Tallahassee "typical."

I'm afraid Quincy is going to have to be relabeled at this point. It sounds too much like typical America right now. When you think about it, though, if racial disharmony defines typical America, then racially motivated lynchings must qualify the participating city as All-America. Way to go, Jasper.

Maybe the label we really should aspire to is "atypical." In an atypical American city, you could ask a person running for commissioner what percentage of the population is a particular color, and the candidate would say, "Dag! I don't know. Is that important?"

If you ever hear of such a place, let me know. And then color me gone.

Tallahassee Democrat – June 25, 1998

The Good News about Bad News

I don't mean to get religious on you, but the needle on the pestilence meter is starting to flirt with the "biblical proportions" mark. The forecast in Florida calls for a fifty-percent chance of raging wildfires, while folks in the Northeast United States are snorkeling to work every morning. All we need now is a good famine, and a plague or two, and 1998 can qualify for the Scourge Hall of Fame. Who is to blame for these disastrous conditions? Some say Mother Nature is the cause, but many experts are blaming the media.

Ah, the media. Whipping boy of the 1990's. Here are some other societal ills caused by the media in recent times: racial tension, violent children, infidelity in the White House, and promulgation or persecution of homosexuality – depending on whose platform is being reported. Other problems traceable to the media include America's loss of family values, teenage pregnancies, low test scores, escalating drug use, and the break-up of the Florida Marlins.

This thing called "media" is nothing but bad news. Which is why the fires and floods, in a strange sort of way, are good news

A funny thing happens when natural disasters occur. The media tends to cover the event, or events. To most of the listening public they tend to over-cover, over-dramatize, and sensationalize the events also. This creates a phenomenon of public hyper-awareness resulting in a paranoia which fuels the belief that the media actually invented the crisis it is reporting.

Are you still with me? I'm almost to the good news.

The good news is that the bad news about fires and floods has kept all comments made by Trent Lott, Reggie White, and the leaders of the Southern Baptist Convention completely out of the media in recent days. If anybody is boycotting or picketing Disney World, I haven't heard about it.

There hasn't been any coverage of racial tensions or violence either. Especially in those areas most affected by the fires and floods. That's probably because when we are trying to save our skins, we don't worry so much about what colors they are. Maybe, with a little help from the elements, we really can get along.

There is nothing like the threat of extinction to put things in perspective. Teenage pregnancies are probably on the wane in the afflicted areas also. Gun owners will be discovering that they can't shoot their way out of surging stormwaters, and that assault rifles are no match for racing infernos.

Residents with flooded basements or burning rooftops are not as likely to be concerned with the appeals process afforded death row inmates. Beleaguered homeowners in these areas may find they are not quite as interested in Bill Clinton's oval office peccadilloes as they are with the disaster relief funding the president will be approving.

The good news about fires and floods is that they make us realize that the real "good news" actually is the media coverage of social turbulence. If we have time to talk about welfare babies and internet pornography it is usually because we are not treading water in our living room or watching our house barbecue all our possessions. Stupid politicians and bigoted religious zealots are just annoying distractions in comparison. They keep us from boredom when the pestilence needle is on low.

So, just to get the record straight, fires and floods are bad news. But they may be necessary reminders that many of the issues we are fretful and frightened of are of little significance in times of true peril. If we could keep this perspective after the flames die and the waters recede, that might really be good news.

Tallahassee Democrat – July 10, 1998

Viva La Ponce!

How does this sound? "Bielecky for Governor." I think I like it. I am going to rely strictly on word-of mouth advertising, so please tell everyone you know to vote for me. After you hear my platform, I mean. I just know you're going to love me.

My primary goal is simple: restoration of the state of Florida to some semblance of what it was when Ponce de Leon discovered it. A little swamp, a lot of bugs, and the kind of beauty that inspires thoughts of living forever.

Here's the plan. First, we shut the gate. No new residents. In fact, the last million people to move here have to go back. If that doesn't work, the previous million have to go also.

How will we know when the population is stable? Easy. When we don't need to widen any more roads. When the average number of students in classrooms is below twenty. We will know we are near the optimum number of citizens when the price of a house in Florida is solely a reflection of the quality of its workmanship and of the size of the lot it is built on.

Speaking of lot sizes, zero-lot lines will be banned forever. Once we've moved out the last three million newcomers (I can feel my constituency growing) we will level every other house so that each resident will have a buffer between themselves and their neighbors. The razed landscapes will be planted with native vegetation to encourage wildlife to populate their former breeding grounds again. Viva la Ponce!

Now, for the tourists. We have to let some in, I suppose. I like a "family only" rule. Friends can come for one week only, and they must pay a hundred dollars a day. This fee will help pay for the deconstruction projects that will be occurring at deserted condominiums along our beaches. Other visitors will be stopped at the gate and given a road map to Arizona.

Once we eradicate the tourists and usher out the four million most recent migrants, we can concentrate on ridding the state of its most noxious pests. First, we kill all the developers. No, wait. Too violent, even if it is fair. So, we let them live, but we give them new jobs. We'll need a few thousand to tend to and protect turtle egg nests along the beaches. Another thousand can start digging gopher tortoise tunnels.

I think you can see the progress we're making here.

But we're just getting started. Let's see if we can make Marjorie Stoneman Douglas smile in her sleep.

I have just one thing to say to Big Sugar. Start the lawnmower! When the last stalk of cane hits the ground, fold up your refineries and get the hell out of here. Take with you every state legislator that you own. The remaining pol can be my lieutenant governor.

While we're down in the southern end of our once pristine peninsula, we will pull the plug on the Florida Keys. Let's disconnect this suffering sanctuary and let time heal the damage we dealt. First, we'll cut the power lines. Then we dismantle the bridges. The estuaries were supposed to be a party playground for lobsters and shrimp, not a urinal for the world's longest Tiki bar.

Moving back up through the central and northern part of the state, we go to work next on polluted rivers and lakes. A lot of money is being spent presently to figure out a way to clean our waters without affecting the polluters too harshly. Wrong, wrong, wrong.

Here is the simplest of propositions. If your industry spews poison into the ponds, you get a padlock on your door. You are hereby grandfathered out, because my grandfather can't stand to see what you have done.

Jobs are not going to be a problem because most of us won't need one. We are going to invite back all the Native American tribes that once called Florida home, and we are going to learn from them how to live efficiently and harmoniously off the land. Those of us who can't fish, hunt, or figure out which roots to eat can become photographers and artists. There should be an incredible market for landscape portraits when the restoration is complete.

Well, that's it. My one and only campaign speech. I expect there will be a groundswell of support from the voting population who were actually born in Florida since they will be the only residents allowed to stay under my Ponce platform of reform.

If you want to be young forever, don't forget to vote.

Tallahassee Democrat – October 8, 1998

The Color of Christmas

There was a song in the late Sixties or early Seventies that went something like this: "Money, money, money, money. MONEEEY!" I don't think there were any other lyrics in the tune. If there were, they were insignificant and unnecessary. I'm perfectly happy chanting this simple little chorus line over and over again. Come on, join me. Money, money, money, money. MONEEEY! Kind of gets in your head, doesn't it?

It's been in my head since I saw how much the Lotto jackpot was worth this week. 55 million American rubles. Wow. It's hard to even put into perspective how much money that is. Let's see, it's more than the total combined yearly salaries of about fifteen hundred public school teachers, but less than half as much as the contract that the post-teenaged basketball player, Kevin Garnett, signed this year.

That doesn't really help, does it? No, the only way to put that much loose change into perspective is to win it. Which is why you should buy a whole lot of Lotto this week. You do feel lucky, don't you?

I know I do. I've done some intensive calculations on my notepad and I have figured out that the odds of matching six numbers are roughly the same as the odds that a Titantic survivor will be discovered tomorrow still bobbing happily in the arctic seas. But I don't care, because I'm singing, baby. MONEEEY!

I'm excited. Marcia Mann, the Lottery Secretary, knew I would be. When the jackpot rolled over to 55 million, she said that this would "... bring tremendous excitement to the game." Marcia knew that the usual measly jackpot of seven or eight million dollars wouldn't raise much interest with stiff competition like Christmas Day looming on the calendar. It's tough to knock off a commercial success like Christmas.

The problem for Marcia, and for the Florida Lottery, is that most people spend their money this week on Christmas stuff. Toys for kids, jewelry for the womenfolk, spark plug wrenches for the menfolk. Some people donate money and gifts to the poor and needy. Happy times for everyone.

But Marcia knows that dangling the double-nickel speed limit number next to a class-climbing word like "million" will divert some of those well-intentioned funds. And it's not like little Joey's stocking has to be empty either. Ten quick-picks may not make the glitter pop off, but hey, everyone knows that good things come in small packages containing high-risk capital ventures. You were going to share some of those tickets, weren't you?

Now, the poor may just have to suffer this year. The twenty bucks I set aside to give to the Santa Claus Fund for Starving Babies suddenly looks a lot better as twenty chances to turn my family members' birthdays into a Limo ride to the Lotto office next Monday. MONEEEY! If I win, every malnourished kid out there gets a Beanie Baby and a Tickle Me Elmo. I promise.

My own kids are too young to share in the excitement, but they will enjoy tearing up the losing tickets as much as they would enjoy any gizmo I could buy them for twice the price. Come to think of it, there's no sense scrimping now. Better give me fifty more for the kids. I'm no Grinch. There is no question, it's the timing of the jumbo jackpot that makes it so special. I'm dreaming of a green Christmas. Lottery spokesperson, Angie Raines, commented on this holiday serendipity. "We can't plan these things. That's why it's so exciting. We'll take it." Angie has the fever. The "we'll take it" sounds a bit cold, indifferent, and businesslike, but I'm sure she meant it in only the most Christmas-spirited kind of way.

Angie is probably just a bit overwhelmed by the fact that even though she works for a state agency, she is now helping direct the campaign for the hottest gift item on the market this year. The Christmas public will be forever thankful. Lotto tickets are the perfect present. We won't have to buy from scalpers. We won't be contributing to third world child labor sweatshops. And we won't be sucked into the commercialization of Christmas by buying from corporate sponsors hawking mainstream wares.

Better yet, we won't have to sing all those Christmas carols this year. We only need to know one line from one song. Come on. Everybody sing. Money, money, money, money. MONEEEY!

December 22, 1998

Food for Thought,
Theory for Dinner

I think I have discovered a new theory that might just make me famous. There are few things in life as exciting as developing your own theory. Einstein must have died from giddiness. So here is my theory: If you take enough dietary supplements, you no longer need to eat. Proof of this theory is that I am no longer hungry. Ever.

I remember thinking to myself when I first started taking a multivitamin: Wow, this thing is the size of a small, green, homegrown banana. The vitamins were a little thick going down, but I never noticed any effect on my caloric intake. Then I started popping vitamin C. Five hundred milligrams of vitamin C comes in a caplet that is roughly about the same size as a popular multivitamin. I was up to two bananas a day.

But in an interview I read, an alternative medicine guru suggested that one thousand milligrams of vitamin C, along with one thousand of vitamin E, would prevent heart attacks and cure dangling participles. My bananas were coming in bunches now.

And then I got sick. I caught the usual cold that takes a hard left at the top of the nasal passage and builds a small fort in a sinus cavity. Man, these things knock me out. But not if I take zinc lozenges in the early stages, before the turning signal comes on.

Zinc is the latest rage in dietary supplements. Scientists recently discovered that in laboratory experiments exposing large chunks of zinc to cold viruses, none of the zinc chunks caught a cold. A theory was born. Another banana was added to my supplement. Three times a day.

This was when I first noticed that my desire to eat was subsiding. Initially, I blamed the disinterest on the taste of the zinc lozenges. Zinc lozenges taste like a Lifesaver with very bad breath. They coat your tongue with a zinc-like substance that makes all food taste similar to tofu. I have never actually eaten tofu, but I have a theory about its taste.

The problem was that zinc alone was not curing my cold. It was stalling the virus just before the fort-building stage, but it wasn't getting rid of it. To get rid of the cold you need Echinacea. Three caplets, three times a day. They come in the usual banana size. I found I was no longer snacking between meals.

The beauty of these supplements is that they are all naturally occurring minerals, herbs, and multivitamin compound conglomerates that the body uses to enhance the immune system and to ward off evil spirits. For example, Echinacea is derived from the Purple Coneflower, commonly grown in gardens tended by alternative medicine gurus. The flower itself is known to attract bees the size of Hyundai's.

All the studies say that ingesting large amounts of Echinacea has no side effects whatsoever. I can only say that since I started taking the purple powder, I sometimes find myself wandering in the garden making strange humming sounds.

If it weren't for the knee surgery, I would probably still eat a light meal now and then. Not that the arthroscopy helped curb my appetite. But two glucosamine sulfate high potency capsules a day ended my craving for lettuce in my salad. I no longer wanted ham on my sandwich. I could still say Ben, or Jerry, but never both together.

I stopped buying groceries when Milk Thistle extract became the final supplement to my diet. Two or more tablets a day for a healthy liver. I'll drink to that. Here's looking up your old hypothesis.

I don't even know how many tablets, capsules, and caplets the size of small, green, homegrown bananas I've eaten today. But I know that I used two eggs over-easy this morning to trap a pesky moth. I had a long conversation at lunch with my foot-long Italian combo, then I tried to set it free in a small wooded area near my house. I played Scrabble with a twenty-two ounce, medium rare Porterhouse for dinner. It beat me by spelling out "mignon," and then took the dog for a walk and never came back.

I'm no scientist. But I am definitely on to something with these dietary supplements. Food has become entirely optional. At least that's my theory.

Tallahassee Democrat – March 5, 1999

Fat Man Blues

A report issued recently by the National Institute of Health said that I was fat. That's a bit bothersome to me. They could have issued a report that said I was ugly and I would have let that pass. Who are they to judge? But they didn't just call me fat, they proved it.

What the kind folks at the NIH have done is develop a mathematical formula that indicates when a person is overweight. The equation goes like this: body weight in pounds multiplied by 703, divided by height in inches squared. The quotient derived from performing these algebraic calisthenics is called your body mass index, or BMI. As a method of determining what kind of shape you are in, this formula has officially replaced standing naked in front of a mirror and turning sideways.

Now for the bad news. If your BMI is 25 or more, you qualify as overweight. A BMI of 30 or more puts you squarely – in a round kind of way – in the obese category. The number to strive for – what Dr. Richard

Atkinson of the American Obesity Association calls the healthiest range – is around 21 or 22. After calculating my BMI, I would guess that these numbers also reflect the age at which the average American last fell into the "healthiest" range.

The thing is, I don't consider myself fat. Okay, so my jeans flinched the last time I reached for them. I figured that was due more to denim shrinkage than to waist expansion. But my BMI number puts me a lot closer to obese than to optimal. I weighed and measured in at a very unsvelte 28 plus. Could you pass the pork rinds, please?

According to some additional calculations I made, fifteen more pounds would garner me a 30 share on the BMI. I almost choked on my cheeseburger.

The report said that being overweight was hazardous to your health. It can put an extra burden on your heart, for one thing. Apparently, the old ticker doesn't work as well when wrapped in bacon. Extra pounds can also cause high blood pressure, diabetes, and shortness of breath during strenuous exercise. I think I'm okay on the first two, but I did get a little winded brushing my teeth this morning.

Now for the really bad news. Let's say I decide I want to be in the "healthiest" range. Let's say I want a BMI of 21. I did some more calculations to determine what my weight would need to be to please the NIH. Did I say that this was really bad news?

Here's the skinny. At six feet, three- and one-half inches tall, I am required to tickle the scales at about one hundred and seventy pounds in order to acquire the desired BMI of 21. Now I don't mean to exaggerate, but at this weight I'll end up on the cover of National Geographic. Ethiopian children will cover their eyes in horror.

The NIH could wire my jaws shut, infect me with dysentery, and put me on a diet that consists only of Ghandi's leftovers and I will never dissipate to one hundred and seventy pounds. As a medically approved guideline, the BMI formula is NUTS. It is apparent that the brain matter of the scientists at NIH is made of the same substance that can be found in the middle of a Moon pie. Yeah, a double-stuffed, chocolate graham – ooh, I'll be right back.

No, you're not going to catch me trying on the Manute Bol line of menswear. The only ribs I want to see are the ones slow-cooking on the mesquite grill with a heavy dose of Danny's Baldheaded slapped on. They can have my Phish Food when they pry it out of my pudgy, lactose-stained fingers.

A hundred and seventy pounds!? If these bozos go on Oprah, the entire food industry is going to sue them. I'm not trying to be uncooperative, but if the NIH doesn't mind, I'll let THEM know when I'm obese. I hope their tofu doesn't go bad while they're waiting.

In the meantime, I'm ordering a double-beef burrito and a side of cheese fries here. I'll burn a few calories when I go channel-surfing with the remote later. I'm just not that vain. End of story. No more National Institute of Health formulas for me.

You don't suppose they really have an Ugly Index, do you?

Tallahassee Democrat – June 26, 1999

Mr. Snub-Nose, and the Exponential Nature of Bad Dreams

Tallahassee Democrat columnist Bill Cotterell previously wrote that more crimes are prevented by handguns than are committed by handguns. Michelle Malkin, a syndicated columnist carried by the Democrat, stated that Americans need look no further than the Revolutionary War to find the essence of our need to continue bearing arms. The Redcoats are still coming? Maybe the Y2K bug hit us pretty hard after all. It just scrambled human brains instead of computers.

Personally, I do not favor private ownership of guns. But the other night, deep into a moonless A.M., I was awakened by a noise. I think I know an intruder when I hear one. So, I reached under my pillow for my fully loaded, snub-nosed revolver with the hollow-point bullets and the guardless trigger. A bit reckless to snooze at Defcon one, I know, but I have to protect what is mine.

You know what I mean. My kids, my wife. My belongings -- not that material things mean anything to me. I'm a liberal for chrissakes. Cotterell understands my readiness. How can you prevent a crime with a handgun if it's not set to shoot? Bang, bang! Helps me sleep.

The best thing about the snub-nosed revolver is its size. You hardly know it's under your pillow. Plus, the hollow-point bullets sound like the ocean if you press your ear very close.

I heard the noise again. I searched for Mr. Snub-Nose, my nostrils flaring like a Blair Witch victim. My fingers stretched longingly for the sanctuary of my gun. My little crime-preventer. My Redcoat repellant.

My hand serpentined the cool side of the pillow, but the seductive comfort of the cold steel was missing. Maybe my wife had it, I thought. She likes to cradle it sometimes when she has a bad dream. I rolled towards her as silent as an intruder just before he makes the noise that wakes you up. I gently frisked her, and she giggled lightly in her sleep, but still no gun.

I thought of shouting to the trespasser, "I have a snub-nosed revolver with hollow point bullets!" but I knew Cotterell and Malkin would make me for a Woody Allen fan if I did.

Then the unthinkable happened. Faster than a 7th grader with a water balloon grudge, the invader bolted into our bedroom. I have to admit I panicked. While frozen in gunless fear I had sudden visions of Jerry

Seltzer cartoons, and I heard Mallard Fillmore quacking derisively at my pinko ineptitude. Charlton Heston force-fed me a handful of soylent green and shouted that he was king of the world, not that snot-nosed DiCaprio.

Then a heavyset, bearded man slapped me, slapped me hard. He could have been anyone, if you live in Tallahassee. "Take this," he drawled, and I found a short-barreled pistol-o-matic in my palm. Drying tobacco juice drippings made the handle sticky, but dadgum, it felt good. I fired seventy-two shots into the heart, lungs, liver, and pancreas of the prowler who had broken and entered. He hit the Berber with a soggy thud, like ground sirloin freshly chucked.

Heston kissed the corpulent, confederate muse right on the mouth. I thought their lips lingered just a bit. Mallard looked at the body and squawked, "Now that's a punchline I can use." I nodded. Overwrought cliché as political commentary, the duck's signature.

Seltzer, wearing a cap that said "Sophomore Forever," was drawing a large chalk outline of a body on my bedroom wall with a caption that said "Your body here if you have triggerlocks." I pointed out that it was a horrible drawing, even for a chalk outline, but he ignored me.

It was my wife who first noticed that the raw hamburger bleeding on the carpet was our youngest son. He always did like to run into our room after a bad dream.

NO! I shouted. I knew the little rugrat couldn't survive seventy-two shots. I looked around. Heston, Seltzer, Mallard, and the burly southern guy were gone. I swooned in anguish.

When I came to, my wife was sleeping. There was no drawing on my wall and I couldn't remember Seltzer's name. Who does, I wondered? There was no child on my carpet. I reached under my pillow and my fingers caressed the hard object reliably waiting. I squeezed it in comfort. Across the room I could make out the fuzzy features of famous actors shooting each other repeatedly on the TV screen. I pulled Old Reliable from under the pillow, pointed it slowly at the television, and pressed the off button.

Tallahassee Democrat – June 19, 2000

The Reasonably High Price of The Mad Gadfly

I'm not actually keeping score, but if memory serves, Eugene Danaher has now been referred to as a gadfly by at least half of Tallahassee's elected officials, by at least one fifth of the Tallahassee Democrat's Editorial Board, and by at least one Tallahassee Democrat "My View" columnist. The Gadfly Gang has not used the word affectionately.

If Danaher is not careful, Jeb Bush may officially anoint him an "evil-doer." Not that Danaher has been associated with al-Qaida. He hasn't even accused Bobby Bowden of coaching dirty football. But Governor Bush has made it his administration's priority to cut government waste, and Danaher's frequently cited sin is precisely that most heinous crime – wasting taxpayer money! One more frivolous ethics complaint by the Mad Gadfly (the high-ranking Mayor of otherwise "All-America" Tallahassee has publicly referred to Danaher as mentally unbalanced) and the city may run out of funding for traffic calming projects, brick crosswalks in the downtown area, or attractive signage advertising the benefits of the penny sales tax.

The recent wrath directed towards Danaher is the result of an ethics complaint he filed against County Commissioner Cliff Thaell. Fellow commissioner, Tony Grippa, who had previously accused Thaell publicly of other uncommissioner-like behavior, immediately requested that Danaher's complaint be withdrawn. Ironically, Grippa's own public accusations of Thaell were the by-product of another Eugene Danaher complaint, against then-commissioner Rudy Maloy, which resulted in formal charges being filed against Maloy, and ultimately, Maloy's ouster. Grippa refused to apologize to Thaell, even though his accusations were never substantiated, and were even, some said, frivolous.

By all accounts, Danaher's current complaint against Thaell is legally unfounded. And this is reportedly not the first time Eugene forgot to check the law before filing a complaint and prancing it immediately in front of the media. However, it should really be pointed out that the Florida Commission on Ethics usually dismisses legally unsupported complaints without a full-fledged investigation, meaning the current Thaell complaint may ultimately cost the taxpayers very little. Yet Danaher's previous complaints against John Thrasher and Gary Yordon led to fines against each, while the fallout from his Maloy complaint was fairly catastrophic.

So, all things considered, why did Democrat Associate

Editor, Bill Berlow, recently devote an entire column to bashing the Mad Gadfly? And why was Reed Mahoney (see: citizen watchdog of citizen watchdogs) singing the blues about Danaher's complaint against Thaell? The Gadfly Gang, of which several have had issues with Thaell, suddenly seem very concerned about protecting Thaell's good name.

Yes, they say, Thaell was slow dancing with a group of local developers at an exclusive local club, and accepting the developers' exclusive cash while partaking of exclusive hors d'eouvres and cocktails. And yes, one of those developers appeared before the County Commission shortly thereafter and obtained Thaell's vote on a development project. So what, says the Gadfly Gang, everything Thaell did was completely legal as the laws are written, and besides, developers with lots of cash for politicians are people too!

Never mind that the laws may be a bit problematic. Is it really legal to allow interested parties to party with elected persons and interest an elected person with cash just before an interested vote is taken? Ahem. Pardon me while I clear the wetlands from my throat.

Personally, I have a much larger issue with Tallahassee's politicos waltzing for dollars with development barons – some of whom have had more lawsuits involving Leon County taxpayer dollars than others – than I do with overzealous citizens who insist on constantly cutting in before the music stops. Besides, the Mad Gadfly has had his share of hits among the misses. Perhaps he just hits too close to home.

Put it this way. Say you had inside information about, say, the tremendous waste and abuse of taxpayer dollars taking place at, say, the Division of Administrative Hearings, which is a government department directly overseen by the same elected public servant who has cut so many other state jobs he may become known as Governor Scissorhands. Say you tried reporting the problem to the right people, in the proper manner, but the result was less than satisfactory. And say that, as a consequence of your whistleblowing, you were immediately exiled from your job.

Who would you call? The Gadfly Gang, or the Mad Gadfly?

All things considered, you might just call Eugene Danaher. He would probably get right on it. And if the cost of the investigation became an issue? Maybe the County Commission could just allocate a small portion of the penny sales tax, and then put the Mad Gadfly's face on signs all over town that say: YOUR TAX DOLLARS AT WORK.

Tallahassee Democrat – January 11, 2002

The Uncomfortable Lightness of Delusional Pasts

On Sunday, February 17, 2002, the Tallahassee Democrat published an opinion column written by Tim Giago, which denounced the use of Native Americans as mascots for sports teams. Giago – identified below his work as an Oglala Lakota - correctly analogized the use of the terms "Redskins" and "Noles" to the offensive use of the word "nigger." In his column, Giago challenged editorial boards of newspapers and politicians across the country with this statement: "What cowardice on the part of the editor of the Washington Post and the elected officials who are in Washington to serve their states and communities. How can they pretend the 'R' word is not as 'offensive' as the 'N' word?"

Good question. But the Editorial Board of the Democrat obviously was not around for that Final Jeopardy query. Because on Tuesday, February 19, 2002, Democrat editors published their own thoughts on racism, and the Florida state of mind. Apparently troubled by the newest unfurling of Old Unglory, the oversized Confederate flag recently raised just Florida of the Georgia border, the opinion expressed was titled: "Dear Visitors: Apologies for Confederate Flag."

I didn't find the opinion below the title to be apologetic at all, even in the most liberal sense of the word. But there was something even more striking in the relatively short tract, something impossible if one had read and understood Giago's piece from just two days before. Two days - not two moons - after Giago eviscerated Tallahassee for its adoption, its virtual embracement of the Seminole tribe as mascots so unimportant as to be reduced to mere "Noles," the largest newspaper in the capital city of Florida signed its name to this statement:

To any and all for whom the display [of the Confederate flag near Georgia] is offensive, we hope you don't assume that modern Florida is a racist state mired in delusions about its past. The great majority of Floridians are comfortable acknowledging our history without having to air brush away its harsh realities.

Is it possible that no author of this incredible paragraph thought of substituting the "Tomahawk Chop" or the infamous "War Chant" as the subject of "the display?" Mr. Giago, you might consider attaching your next essay to a flaming spear. That, we pay attention to here in "Seminole Nation." Fifty-yard line please, and don't forget the feathered headdress.

I do agree, though, that we Floridians don't air brush

away the harsh realities of our past. No refinement allowed. We prefer crude applications of "war paint" while blundering forth in blissful ignorance of historical misdeeds.

Are we really "comfortable acknowledging our history?" How many of us have the foggiest notion of the history of Florida Native Americans? As it turns out, the "Indian Removal Act" was not what happened when Florida State's football team played the Gators last year; it was a law signed by Andrew Jackson that led to the systematic displacement and extermination of Native Americans in the eastern U.S. And Oklahoma was not just the team that beat FSU in back-to-back bowl games a few years back; it's the state where over three thousand Florida Native Americans were forcibly removed to in the 1830's.

Those are just a couple of small details I picked up on the Seminole Tribe of Florida website (seminoletribe. com/index.shtml). Here's a quote the tribe forgot to hit with the air brush: "The Seminole people - men, women, and children, were hunted with bloodhounds, rounded up like cattle, and forced onto ships that carried them to New Orleans and up the Mississippi." Editors, are you still comfortable?

Mr. Giago's thoughtful, passionate, and persuasive writings on the topic of Natives Americans as sports mascots are published by the Tallahassee Democrat several times each year. But it would not be overstating the obvious to posit that Giago is not making much headway. And it wouldn't be much of a limb to go out on to suggest that the Democrat's Editorial Board ain't exactly jumping on his bandwagon. That's fine. Lipservice is not illegal.

But the "Dear Visitors" opinion ought to be. The Confederate flag at issue is flying on private property; the Tomahawk Chop, and white kids dyed and costumed as "Chief Osceola" are sponsored by a state university. The performance of the "war chant" at Doak Campbell Stadium by seventy-five thousand plus fans can be witnessed on any given autumn Saturday by millions of visitors and non-visitors alike.

Better tell those folks again, editors, in case they were reading Tim Giago while you were talking: please don't assume modern Florida is a racist state mired in delusions about its past.

February 19, 2002

THE WOODPECKER FAN CLUB

"Changing places at the table doesn't fool the cards."

- Tom Robbins, Still Life With Woodpecker

THE EMAILS

The following are emails written when I was teaching high school at John I. Leonard in 1993 - 1994. I suppose The Woodpecker Fan Club was a blog before blogs, but I wasn't trying to invent anything, I was just trying to stay out of trouble and entertain the troops at the same time. It was the earliest days of email, and JIL's email system was in-school only. Naturally, I abused it as soon as I got my hands on it. The Woodpecker Fan Club was the result of a scolding I received for authoring a whimsical email and sending it to the entire school's staff and teachers. The email was based on actual events. It went like this:

To: ALL TEACHERS
From: B. Bielecky
Date: November 19, 1993

Subject: **NIRVANIC UTOPIA**

AS I WAS ESCORTING TWO TRUANTLY DISTRESSED GENTLEMEN TO THE DISCIPLINE TERMINAL THIS MORNING I COULDN'T HELP BUT NOTICE THE TREES JUST OUTSIDE THE CAFETERIA. THEY ARE IN A STATE OF SPLENDIFEROUS BLOOM; SIMPLY MAGNIFICENT. NATURALLY I STOPPED FOR A LONGER LOOK (IN SPITE OF THE PROTESTATIONS OF MY TWO WALKING PARTNERS) IN ORDER TO FULY APPRECIATE THIS WONDER OF NATURE. AS I GAZED AND SLIPPED INTO A

PEACEFUL TRANQUILITY A SMALL BLACK DOG WITH A PURPLE TONGUE JOGGED BY.
IT WAS AT THIS MOMENT THAT IT ALL MADE SENSE.

Immediately after this was sent I was admonished by the school's tech administrator to send my vagaries of thought to selected "groups" only, not to "All." Ok. First, I had to find a group. The following is my initiation email welcoming like-minded teachers at the high school to join the WFC, followed by the random, abstract, and whimsical emails I would post to the group when I wasn't chasing smokers through hallways. I think we had about seventy members by the time I left JIL for law school. Which was likely a larger audience than my columns ever attracted.

To: A Select Group
From: B. Bielecky
Date: January 11, 1994

Subject: Esoteric Psychobabble

Welcome!   You are now an unofficial member of the Woodpecker Fan Club – unofficial because nothing official transpires on this underground network. You have been selected on the basis of your beauty, brains, and wit. And because you have been detected to elicit a propensity towards the surreal, sublime, and generally metaphysical happenings. Not exactly Galtesque, but Bernard Mickey Wrangle would surely approve.

Beginning sometime soon you will receive intermittent, random ramblings on subjects ranging from extracting gold from the ocean for profit to how to get a tan on the dark side of the moon. Stuff you can really sink your mind into – or that you can just ignore. There are no rules in the Woodpecker Fan Club, although you may correct bad grammar or admonish rude comments at your discretion.

All topics are open for discussion, including, but not limited to the volatile ones. New members are welcome. Initiation fees and dues are waived forever. No secret knocks, handshakes, passwords or other silliness is required. We will wear no identifying colors or hang out in any particular place – the world is our oyster, and if we sprinkle enough hot sauce on it, it may not be poisonous.

If at any time you find that your life would be a better place to be if you were not a member of the Woodpecker Fan Club, simply contact me the usual way and you will be released of your duty immediately. What is your duty? As a member in good, bad, or indifferent standing it is your duty to either read or quickly erase without reading any messages that henceforth transpire. You must either enjoy, hate, or shake your head quizzically if you do read. You must either answer or not answer. You must either wonder about the meaning of life or you must know what the meaning of life is.

As Alice Cooper once said, "welcome to my nightmare." You are on your own from now on – as you have always been. Party on, Garth. And pass the tabasco, please.

To: Woodpecker Fan Club
From: B. Bielecky
Date: January 18, 1994

Subject: Helter Shelter

Shake, Rattle, and roll. Even natural disasters have a ready-made soundtrack, and they are cause for pause in our day to reflect on our fragile existence and ponder our eternal quest to put a roof over our heads: shelter, one of the lower rungs of Maslow's Hierarchy. The problem is, how can we be sure that roof won't end up falling on our head? Maybe we should reevaluate and strive for self-actualization first and put shelter on the top rung where we're not supposed to reach anyway.

Mr. Haney first, then goes Harry Nilsson. Do the deaths of obscure entertainers usually happen in threes? Nilsson makes me think of Ratso Rizzo shaking off the cold and trying to stay warm dancing to the Florida orange juice song.

Guns don't kill people, thirteen year olds kill people – NRA slogan or title of a poem found on a bathroom wall? Discuss . . . I dreamt the other night that I was sleeping and having a bad dream. My doctor thinks I'm not getting enough fiber in my diet.

To: Woodpecker Fan Club
From: B. Bielecky
Date: January 20, 1994

Subject: **Chicken Lips and Ink Dots**

Kenny Rogers ad Boston Chicken announced simultaneously yesterday that they would not be expanding their existing stores to accommodate drive-thru chicken as previously planned. Instead, in a business decision reflecting contemporary society, both franchises plan to begin marketing drive-by chickens. Employees will motor through neighborhoods in mini-vans and fire rounds of chicken at unsuspecting residents. Direct hits will be paid for by a special federal government fund. A White House spokesperson said, "Hey as long as the chicken is skinless." Experts say this may save the government billions of medical dollars annually if it catches on. Bill Clinton failed a Rorschach test immediately after giving his approval.

To: Woodpecker Fan Club
From: B. Bielecky
Date: February, 1994

Subject: **Where Yesterday Went**

It's not important really, the passage of time. What is important is how we mark that passage. Do we lament the disappearance of our youth or celebrate our status?

Should we not leap into life each morning and mark each day with our scent like a grizzly that claws and scratches the tallest tree and then sprays it with his personalized cologne? After all each day is a victory, isn't it? Should we not notch our bedposts for every day that we survive? Because who knows when this experiment will conclude?

So yes, there are days when we feel like the silver mullet as he makes his mindless trek south for the winter, bluefish attacking from below, pelicans dive bombing from above, fishermen casting nets from shore, and to survive all this merely means a lonely death on a sandy floor where the crabs wait and always take the eyes first. But notch that bedpost just the same and drink the air like the elixir of life that it is. Mark your passage well. Happy birthday, Frosty.

To: Woodpecker Fan Club
From: B. Bielecky
Date: February 23, 1994

Subject: Munch on This

While the world threw up its collective arms and cried out in a sonic silent scream (dogs everywhere perked their ears and wrinkled their noses into the wind) over the theft of Munch's classic painting, "The Scream", another significant heist was pulled off. Scarcely noticed in the turmoil was the pilferage of another Munch classic, "The Stare." This priceless portrait of school principal Luke

Thornton was discovered to be missing several days after "The Scream" was stolen in that daring museum raid. There are no clues as to when or how "The Stare" was removed from the front office of John I. Leonard High School. Top security officials and art experts believe the same persons are responsible for both thefts and say that while "The Scream" was priceless, owning both pieces makes the artwork twice as priceless. Mathematicians are scrambling to find a formula that properly illustrates this much pricelessness.

To: Woodpecker Fan Club
From: B. Bielecky
Date: February 25, 1994

Subject: Git Fidler

The weekend looms before us, as large as a sumo wrestler about the enter the hot tub you're occupying. Happy hour approaches in fifty minute increments marked by the ebb and flow of our illustrious student bodies. For whom do these bells toll? Well it tolled the other day for Papa John Creach, and I submit the first toast in his honor today. Papa John was a senior citizen rock and roll violinist who once played with Jefferson Starship. If "Red Octopus" is on the jukebox we'll have to cue up "Git Fidler" and bid a fond adieu.

The Greek fest has Ouzoed its way into town – a fine place to enjoy a slice of lamb and a little baklava, and Spalding

Gray visits the Duncan Theater tomorrow night to deliver a meandering monologue on the strangeness of life and the complications that being alive cause us.

Don't stay in the hot tub too long. See you at Jack's. Party on, Garth.

To: Woodpecker Fan Club
From: B. Bielecky
Date: March 4, 1994

Subject: March 5th

It's the same everywhere – you exit the birth canal and the judge is waiting, bang bang, he says with the gavel, "I sentence you to life." And so it begins, and we start our journey, often feeling like a salmon heading upstream, never knowing if a grizzly fresh out of hibernation is waiting around the corner, but knowing we will take that corner anyway. Probably on two wheels. Where are we going? And what will we do when we get there? Well, maybe the Townes van Zandt said it best, "Living's mostly wasting time, and I've wasted my share of mine, but it never feels too good . . ." I don't know where we're going, but I do know you hit a toll booth on the mountain once a year. This is a good place to stop and take a deep breath, look back at all the grizzlies you skated by and check out the view. Time to carve another notch in the sunset and celebrate your own personal anniversary.
Happy Birthday Mom!!!!!!!!!!!

To: Woodpecker Fan Club

From: B. Bielecky

Date: March 22, 1994

Subject: If We Weren't All Crazy.....

I'm mellow as hell and I'm not going to take it anymore
. . . if swallows were woodpeckers would they fly to
the Hawaiian instead of Capistrano to celebrate the
vernal equinox?

Ah springtime, flowers blooming, birds returning from
their winter vacation, and the sound of children shooting
each other on the playground.

Daylight savings time will be forced up on us soon. Who
invented this? Somebody wanted it to be 8:00 p.m. when it
was 7:00 p.m.? How can this be legal? I mean, I want it to
be Friday when it is Thursday, okay? In fact, I want it to
be June when it is May. Why don't we just skip ahead ten
years and check out the 21st Century? Who's in charge
here anyway? March madness – down right ubiquitous
phrase, I think . . . watch out for Marquette in the SE . . . .

To: Woodpecker Fan Club
From: B. Bielecky
Date: March 24, 1994

Subject: Helter Skelter

I watched Groundhog Day last night for the seventeenth day in a row.

Going to see Jackson Browne tonight. As Don Meredith used to say, "Music to slash your wrists by". Wouldn't it be great when you had a relationship go bad to write entire albums of music about it? And people would buy it?

Charles Manson looks like he still has those bad hair days. I kept wishing he would brush the bangs out of Diane Sawyer's eyes and make her watch stop.

Kimberly Mays switched parents. A trial that probably costs millions, a landmark, groundbreaking judicial decision, then the kid gets grounded for a week and overturns the whole deal. I say she should have to pay for the trail out of her allowance.

To: Woodpecker Fan Club
From: B. Bielecky
Date: March 25, 1994

Subject: Silence of the Woodpeckers

So I'm worried about you guys. It's been very quiet on the woodpecker telegraph lately. My email is getting too much official business and not nearly enough unofficial nonsense. We're not taking ourselves too seriously again are we? We haven't tried to work the last 42 days without playing hooky, have we? Okay, here's my top ten list of things to do to snap out of this lethargy:

10. Drink three jalapeno martinis and then explain the "Sylvia" cartoon to your next door neighbor.

9. Go to Kravis center for a cultural awakening and jut near the end of the show, during a quiet part, yell, "HOOT THERE IT IS" as loud as you can.

8. Write a letter to the editor comparing political importance of Louis Farrakhan's speeches to the collective work of the Three Stooges. Nuk. Nuk. Nuk.

7. Sneak into the Principal's office and make a lengthy 1-900 phone call.

6. Rent the video "Kalifornia", then go out and pick up a hitchhiker.

5. Get a can of spray paint and write "Kids kant spel" in the halls near your room.

4. Buy a gallon or two of orange juice, then return any copies of Rush Limbaugh books you can find and demand your money back.

3. Do a security check, go to the Norton Art Gallery, grab a Picasso and run like hell.

2. Put on a Dick Vitale mask, grab the microphone and do a play by play on the next fight in the cafeteria – ITS SHOWTIME, BABY!!!

1. Make plans to be at the next Woodpecker Happy Hour, Thursday March 31 at the Hawaiian on the beach immediately following the planning day!

To: Woodpecker Fan Club
From: B. Bielecky
Date: March 28, 1994

Subject: Babylon Sisters

It's a Santa Ana wind blowing, and it's making me nervous. Or maybe it's just a full moon hangover. Maybe it's the scent of spring break wafting through the corridors. It just seems like school is a cross between "Catch-22" and "One Flew Over the Cuckoo's Nest" lately. Was Jim Morrison doing too much acid or was he really a shaman visionary of the 1990s when he sang, "All the children are insane"?

The search for the meaning of life continues, as elusive as the lost ark or the holy grail ever were. It's out there somewhere, riding the tide on the tail of El Nino. When it finds me, I'm going to buy a big hat and rent a permanent space at the tiki bar and explain it to all my friends. I think I will practice on Thursday.

To: The Woodpecker Fan Club (Each name now listed alphabetically)

From: B. Bielecky

Date: April 21, 1994

Subject: Lonesome Woodpecker

"There is no evidence that life should be taken seriously" – Anonymous

The woodpecker fan club lives! (Though it may be an endangered species). The new email system is ugly. I am sorry. I mean, look at all those names – I feel a draft in the email. It is hard to wax philosophical when you're exposed like this. Well, I guess you know you've been living in the modern world too long when you start yearning for the old-fashioned email. I do like the F9 button, though. More options – should be an attachment to life. Just hit that baby, scan down to planets and hit "friendlier". But what if you ended up on planet Singapore? Bruce Lee waiting for you with a big cane pole to insure your friendliness. Kinda makes your butt twitch just thinking about it, doesn't it? Way too serious for me. Never get off the boat, baby!

To:　　Woodpecker Fan Club
From:　B. Bielecky
Date:　May 9, 1994

Subject: If I had a Rocket Launcher
Good evening woodpeckers, it's been too long.

A bit of order seems restored to the world lately. The caning is completed, Munch's "Scream" has been safely returned, the Heat properly stumbled out of the playoffs, Grade Nite and prom are both in the bag, and the final remnants of Sunfest are oozing out of livers like toxic waste in a neighborhood landfill seeping into the aquifer. Oh yeah, and the white guys lost in South Africa. Get up, stand up. Kaos has been thwarted again. Fine Job, 86.

Unless you're worried about the resurgent popularity of heroin as the drug of choice for today's youth. Or the deal in Rwanda where soldiers are hacking up people with machetes like they were sugar cane in Pahokee. Closer to home, little kids are coming to "show and tell" armed and dangerous. The NRA can only beam with pride as their motto "A gun for every man, woman and child" comes increasingly closer to fruition. And Donahue is supposed to be emceeing a live execution on TV soon. I tip my hat to Paddy Chayefsky, and as I scratch my head in wonderment I hear the monotone of Paul Harvey say, "Page two . . . ."

To: Woodpecker Fan Club
From: B. Bielecky
Date: May 17, 1994

Subject: Hardening of the Woodpecker
So, no more margarine for me. I'm eating my toast dry now. I just inject beef fat right into my heart.

Where should we send the troops?   Haiti? Bosnia? Rwanda? Detroit? The 200 building? Sometimes I just feel like bombing everyone until there's peace on earth.

John Bobbitt was arrested for beating up his fiancée. This is not a smart man. Let's hope the woman had previously acquired a complete set of Ginzu kitchenware.

Ok, raise your hand. How many people really want to see Donahue host a live execution on TV? (Is that the ultimate oxymoron or what?) I only want to see it if Bevis and Butthead get to perform it...

To: Woodpecker Fan Club
From: B. Bielecky
Date: June 3, 1994

Subject: Taxi!!!

I stopped Travis Bickle in the hallway this morning.

"You talkin' to me? he asked. You talkin' to me? I don't

see anyone else here, you must be talkin' to me."

I glanced briefly at the other students crowding past us. Travis's eyes were darting frenetically, like a small animal in a trap. Firecrackers exploded just behind me, but I kept my cool.

Travis poked himself in the chest and inflated a little more. "You talking to me?"

"No, Travis," I said, "actually I was speaking to that little black dog with the purple tongue. We're both big on the new Jimmy Dale Gilmore album."

Travis looked confused, but somehow pacified as he slowly walked away.

"Hey Travis," I yelled after him, "have you seen the flowers blooming in the courtyard?"

Travis went to class, passed a final exam and became a national hero.

To: Woodpecker Fan Club
From: B. Bielecky
Date: June 8, 1994

Subject: Time For Me to Fly

"The best thing you ever did for me, is to help me take my

life less seriously. It's only life after all." – Indigo Girls

Well, Woodpeckers, it looks like this big tree is all hollowed out. Time to find some new bark to go bang on. Something in a large oak maybe, in north Florida, with lots of Spanish moss.

Ah, The Woodpecker Fan Club. The unofficial underground network founded on the principles of pretzel logic as they apply to the esoteric philosophies of John Galt, Bernard Mickey Wrangle, Nietzsche, and Tom Sawyer. Long live the Woodpecker Fan Club!

I'm going to miss my email. You guys are as priceless as an Edvard Munch "Scream" (or "Stare") any day. Think of me occasionally next fall as you scroll through the official school business that incessantly immolates this otherwise fine place to hang out. Remember to keep the Tabasco handy – there's still some bad oysters on the market.

And when you're feeling a little uptight, and there's too many grim faces in the halls, and you're tired of suspension lists, bus changes, and ESOL points news, peck out some nonsense on your computer and send it to a bunch of people. Somewhere out there a Woodpecker will either read it or erase it, smile or shake its head quizzically, love it or hate it; or just meet you at happy hour and explain the meaning of life to you. Au revoir, Garth. Party on . . .

POETRY

"There is no single particular noun
for the way a friendship.
stretched over time, grows thin,
then one day snaps with a popping sound."

- Tony Hoagland (Special Problems in Vocabulary)

Bill Bielecky

The Lonely Door

It was a night, the night we met
To meet again, as if before
To ride the tide of passion, yet
Keep one eye on the lonely door

And as the door swings ever shut
Don't let the lock be turned
On hearts confused and silent, but
Aware of what's been learned

Knock and knock upon that door
It seems so open wide.
But just as in the times before
There is a lonely side

Where love is thrashed and thrown about
Tossed upon the floor
I see again the lingered doubt
My address on the lonely door

There is no hope beyond the room
where love is made once more
Lie quietly amid the gloom
And close the lonely door

11/10/90

Silent Tides

Far below the surface
There runs a silent tide,
Sweeping your emotions
To a secret place they hide.
Past the heart, and troubled soul
To a place no one has seen,
You love and hate and love again
And live somewhere in between.

The river flows so black and cold
Beneath a levee so unkind,
Filling you with hopelessness
For the life you cannot find.

Eternal youth and happiness
Once sprang from this well,
But time erodes with passage
The secrets you won't tell.
Don't tell me now, it's far too late
To share forbidden pain.
Don't burden me with silent tides
That leave this bloodless stain.

The darkness of your eyes
Is like an ocean of despair.
They keep a lonely vigil
For the life that is not there.

1/7/91

Bill Bielecky

Manuscripts of Life

This manuscript of life you wrote
Is not the one for me.
I'll travel far and stay at home
If you'll just let me be.
Embrace the sky, kiss the sea,
Leave this tiny earth,
For a destination's universe
To learn my secret worth.
Beyond the space that stretches out
Where none of us can see,
I'll reach inside and light the torch
Of my own galaxy.

The answers now that sate my soul
Are not the ones of youth.
The questions asked can never quench
The thirst of troubled truth.
For though it's told and written down,
Who penned this mighty tale?
And if I never heard this myth
Would it be just as well?
And if I'm here, and then I'm gone
And never learned what you had taught,
Will sleeplessness be rendered
By the lessons that I fought?

I don't believe the fabled words
Of wonder and sublime.
Enlist instead the quiet truths

That qualify my time.
And reach beyond the latitudes
Of comfort and control,
Far beyond the clutches
Of my spirit and my soul.
There at last it comes to light,
An answer to my being.
Ambiguous, this faded print
Whose images are fleeing.

2/21/91

Bill Bielecky

Death of Number Twenty-Two

Doubt like shrapnel flies about,
Indecision haunts the past.
Move the pawn, protect the king,
Ignore the languid pallor cast.
Run like lichens from the light,
Bear the scars of this foray.
Surrender, drenched in robes of madness
Housing lobes of deep decay.
Answer calls of distilled friends,
Pockets full of time they borrow.
Refuge is the unsafe harbor,
Hide in shrouded sheets of sorrow.

2/11/91

Welcome to the Neighborhood

Relax your bones in altered states,
Amid the palms plucked from the wood.
Here love and laughter fill the plates,
Welcome to the neighborhood.

Waterfalls of reddened wines
Elicit tales of fabled lore.
Don't stand in unattended lines,
Walk backwards through this humored door.

And gorge on feasts of disarray
Prepared within this sensual college.
Leave behind your troubled day,
And pass the pipe of higher knowledge.

Convene inside these jungled fences
To marinate the ties that bind.
Obliterate the common senses,
Join this sect of life reclined.

And lounge with surrealistic birds
That dance in place misunderstood.
Stroll slowly through these gardened words,
Welcome to the neighborhood.

4/9/91

Bill Bielecky

Hedonistic Snapshots

A tawny stretch of buxom youth
Like an oasis in the desert heart,
Where its seduction is a flirting breeze
That rivers through the grains of sand
To find the timeless beauty fading
And love is like a metaphor.

The fiery flesh burns silken hair
Into the image of desperate forests
Or irrigated fields of hope
Where dreams are sown
But harvest moons are blue,
Eclipsed by dreams that never end.

Variegated eyes reflect immortal thoughts
From nomadic generations
Drunk on tasteless wines,
With their air-brushed aspirations,
But never see the emptiness
When these hedonistic snapshots
Crumble at their feet.

Venetianed silhouettes outline shapely prisms
Dancing lightly towards the distance
Where the view is always hungry
For the closeness of a touch
That would never raise the flesh
If there was a rainbow's end.

5/7/91

Unfiltered Children

See unfiltered children work
With dialect of unconcern
Tattoo their tests with scarlet pens
And wonder if they ever learn.
Graffitied minds wander aimless,
Blankened by igneous maps.
With disenchanted energy
They labor through their sleepless naps.

Projectiles fly with bored abandon
And graze the innocent observer.
Fists are clenched to flaunt disdain
And chaos reigns with lightninged fervor.
They roam the aisles, festooned with fury,
Subtracted from a life of fear.
What punishment can fit their crime?
There's no administration here.

Where will they go when they escape,
These products of some unknown quotient?
A homeless world awaits with hunger
To drown them in an unnamed ocean.

5/20/91

Bill Bielecky

Some Dream

Sultry passions, finally realized,
Linger in the mind.
Slow-motion love with all-star teams
Chastefully refined.
Familiar scents cologne the thoughts
With wistful recollection.
Painted lips and perfumed eyes
That glance in this direction.
Enchanted ladies loiter here,
Telephoned by somnolence.
They leave behind a pensive heart
That worries of its innocence.

6/10/91

The Jaded One

She came in different colors,
Not looking for romance,
Like Pinatubo sunsets,
Like this was her last chance.
She was a golden yellow
With Harlem eyes I could undress,
And caramel colored third world skin
That screamed for my caress.

But she kept her distance,
As if we were in love.
As if she somehow knew
What we were thinking of.

Her untamed hair lay in trestles
Across autumn-leaf thin shoulders,
To bridge the miles between Malaysia
And lovers dressed like soldiers.
In forbidden skirts that sliced
Like guillotines of denim fun,
She laughed with misplaced innocence,
Like she was the jaded one.

When her lips had glanced off mine
They left a purple stain,
Like overripened berries
Washed in a gentle rain.

3/4/92

Bill Bielecky

Abstract Thoughts On Random Days

I fall so deep into this thought
I submerge.
Breathing is not necessary
When I chase the dream.

I think of where I have not been,
And know she does not know me.
If she never finds me
Will you introduce me
To her friend?

There is a fish I've never caught,
I plan the day we'll meet.
The line will smoke,
The reel will shriek.
There will be one less thing
I need to do.

Patience is the car I drive,
But I park in yellow zones.
I make calendars with tickets
They place upon my window.

I took some pictures of my past,
But still I could not change.
I studied angles, shadows, light,
silhouettes.
Then someone stole my film.

Chin Music

I think there is a thought
That I have not discovered.
I gaze up at the surface
But I know that it's not there.
Breathing is not necessary
When I chase the dream.

I didn't see them play the game,
But I saw the instant replay.
It did not matter who had won,
The game was surely fixed.

The show was almost over
When I finally found my seat.
I was so deep into this thought
I never saw the end.

9/12/91

Bill Bielecky
Life on the Half-Shell

I remember when you thought you knew me
As I sat upon the shallow reef.
Then you watched in discombobulation
When I swam across the shelf's abyss,
Ignoring all the books and tables,
And dove the wall's receding light.

I searched black coral for narcosis
But nitrogen was not in season,
So I surfaced in this sober state
With bloodshot eyes from blended cactus,
And when you didn't recognize me
I knew I couldn't make your flight.

But we had dinner reservations
For two, or more, at Amadeus,
Where we appetized on roast iguana
And drank a toast to stark confusion.
Then while I sipped on licorice wine
I planned my uncontrolled descent
Into caves of moray eels
Whose telephones are never listed.

And I watched you use a thoughtless fork
To pick the flesh from bones
Of fish that I had fed that day.
You couldn't know where I had been
Or guess where I would go,

Chin Music

Or understand the secret wish
Of every oyster that lays shucked
Upon a bed of shaven ice.

10/16/91

Bill Bielecky

the nihilistic hostess

she smiled as she greeted me
but her eyes were so forlorn
they whispered of a silent wish
that they never had been born

* * *

she sat me at the corner table
near the nuclear reactor
right beside an empty cross
inscribed 'god is not a factor'

then she pointed to the doomsday menu
tattooed across her legs
it offered sautéed baby seals
and omelets of green turtle eggs

she inhaled from carcinogens
as my order was completed
she said that i could take her home
when the ozone was depleted

then she took the seat across from me
and told me several lies
about a happy childhood
and how she never cries

she left to serve my dinner
one course at a time
the soup d'jour was oil spill
garnished with a lime

Chin Music

she brought irradiated pesticides
supplied by bankrupt farms
she told me if i had a taste
i'd father children with no arms

then she grimly served my main entree
a grinning fish upon a plate
a speargun shaft ran through its head
she said it looked like fate

there are people starving everywhere
so she didn't let me finish
she said that the apocalypse
would help my appetite diminish

as i sipped my after-dinner drink
she swallowed twenty pills
sliced laterally along her wrists
and said she'd pay my bill

then she wished me a good evening
with eyebrows crossed in sorrow
she said that she would save my table
if i came back tomorrow

* * *

i met her at a restaurant
this funny little girl
she smiles for a living
while she worries for the world

10/17/91

Bill Bielecky

The Softest Death of All

Lying on my back
In a sea of flaxen grass,
I looked up at an empty sky,
So blue, and pure,
And waiting to be ambushed.
This was life
When I was young

A whisper of a cloud
That seemed ten years away,
Tried to pull me towards it,
But I pressed
Back to the earth,
Secure in my reluctance,
And dreamed a dream instead

From this prone position
I watched with studied eyes
As turkey buzzards soared
In ever softer circles,
Hypnotizing me,
And disguising their true menace,
Recognizing me
As carrion for future meals

Life was illustrated then
By streaks of jet plane smoke
That died
The softest death of all.

Chin Music

Hardened lines
That split the sky
As if they made a difference,
Then slowly billowed,
Fading,
To disappear without a trace
As if they never lived

It was an azure classroom
Of fighter planes,
And vultures,
And cirrus invitations
That never seemed to last.
It was a world
That granted me
Exemption from these subtle fates.
This was life
When I was young

1/28/92

Bill Bielecky

There Goes the Neighborhood

I found myself within this circle,
It was never quite complete.
I'm clueless to the missing link,
I still live on this street.

And though my address hasn't changed,
The view is not as pretty.
I once lived in the neighborhood,
I now live in the city.

And if it's not the way we'd choose,
It's how we live our lives.
Put double locks upon our doors
And watch for friendly knives.

For there is no home that's not for sale,
No circle that's unbroken.
There's no way to take back unsaid words
Once they have not been spoken.

So I'll walk along this sad circumference,
This oft-aborted trail,
I'll pass by those familiar faces
On this path I know so well.

6/3/92

Drive-By Bukowskis

Listening to the Drive-By Truckers
With their Bukowski lyrics

Notice I didn't say Bukowskiesque
He wouldn't roll over in his grave at that
He wouldn't waste that kind of time
Or like the cliche
He would just reach out of the earth
And choke me

Bukowski said his dad beat him
Until all his pretension was gone
I wonder who beat the Truckers

Bukowski didn't play with metaphors
Neither do the Truckers
Much
They both make you feel
Like a pussy
For using metaphors and similes

But then
There is Tom Robbins
After all

4/29/06

Bill Bielecky
Brevity

Fifteen million years ago
A rhinoceros roamed the earth.
They found his bones just yesterday
Near a turnpike in the dirt.
He was resting there quite comfortably,
Bleached white as alabaster,
Still wondering why the living years
Passed by him so much faster.

Some little man became much bigger
When he etched his ego onto glass.
Somehow he never figured out
How to make his image last.
He disappeared, as all men do,
And no one really cared.
He left the world no worse or better
For having once been there.

A guilty woman worried
As she sped her way through life,
Should she stop, enjoy this day,
Or become a better wife?
It never once occurred to her
As she cried out to the Lord,
This is all there really is,
There is no great reward.

Chin Music

Where is it that they rush to
As they fly through these fine years?
No one will even look for them
For fifteen million years.

4/15/92

Bill Bielecky

Scars Upon The Earth

Every highway carved between the mountains
Is a scar upon the earth.
All that pavement, all those wires,
scars upon the earth.
Every tree cut down
And every pipeline laid
Every ditch ever dug
Is just a scar upon the earth.

Every bomb that ever dropped
And plane that ever crashed
Every ship that ever sank
Every war that never ends
Is just another scar upon the earth.

The planet spins and heals itself
It takes longer every time.
Now there are scars upon the scars
Upon the planet earth.

Every tyrant, President,
Every single Pope
Are all just scars upon the earth.
Every headline in the news
Every man in jail
Every politician
every judge
And every lie they ever told
Was a scar upon the earth.

Chin Music

The poisons spilled into the water
Every fish they ever killed
Every bird that never flies again
Is a scar upon the earth.
Every woman ever beaten
By every single man,
Every child ever harmed
And every time he overcame
Is a scar upon the earth.

Every pill that gets you through your day
Every book you never read
Every bible ever preached
Any money ever taxed
Every animal in every cage
And every person in every house
Is another scar upon the earth.

The world is just an island
Too beautiful for us
We couldn't stand it anyway
Until every corner had been touched
By a scar
Upon the earth.

10/7/05

Bill Bielecky

Plexiglass Airlines

A bird flew into the plexiglass today
Two birds actually
A few days ago two others
Or the same two
Flew into the same plexiglass
I guess they can't see it
Or imagine that it's there
And a Hummingbird did the same
The first two birds
And the Hummer
Woke up nicely and flew away
Eventually
But today bird number one was just dead
Bird number two was out for a while
But it finally woke up
I took the feeders down
But what if there was plexiglass
Where we flew our planes

3/5/17

ABOUT THE AUTHOR

Bill Bielecky was born in West Palm Beach, where he grew up watching the demise of south Florida. He later attended Florida State University's creative writing program, and graduated with a degree in English in 1981. He spent the next nine years, as many English majors do, in the restaurant business, including as owner-operator of a small restaurant in West Palm Beach from 1986 – 1990. His writing credits during this time included several letters to the editor of the Palm Beach Post, and a couple of songs he cannot find.

After selling the restaurant he became a substitute teacher, and obtained a degree in Education from Florida Atlantic University. He was hired at John I. Leonard High School as a Crisis Intervention Teacher in 1992. During his years at JIL he coached the boys and girls swim teams (because nobody else would take the job), was co-sponsor of the Junior class, assisted the yearbook staff, and chased a lot of kids suspected of smoking all over campus (he never caught any, and some teachers accused him of not really trying).

He left teaching in 1994 to attend law school at Florida State University (he cannot explain why), and stayed in Tallahassee to watch the demise of north Florida. He opened a solo law firm in 1998 and has practiced in the area of Consumer Protection Law ever since. He has sued a lot of car dealers, and other Tin Men along the way. He intends to write a novel depicting the scam artists of the modern business world, the lonely few lawyers who hound them, the morally corrupt lawyers who defend them, and the judges and legislators who let them go and protect them.

Bielecky currently lives in Tallahassee, Florida, with his wife. They have two sons who now have to pretend they read everything in Chin Music. Including the poems.

The author. When he was young.